# Mommy Can Buy Happy Nest

# DEDICATION

I dedicate this book to my only daughter,
**SOPHIA MARGARETTE SANTOS**

*"Sophia, my firstborn and my only girl.*
*Because of You,*
*I became a MOM for the first time.*
*Know that you're accepted, treasured, and loved*
*for who you are!*
*I thank God that He's given me YOU.*
*Who you are now and tomorrow,*
*I'm simply proud."*

*With so much love,*
***Mommy***

# ACKNOWLEDGMENTS

To my **Creator,** thank you for giving me a wonderful journey that brought me to my desired destination. You are simply an awesome God!

To my very supportive and loving husband, **Christopher Santos**, thank you for always being there for me and for believing in me. You're the best!

To my precious treasures, my four kids: **Sophia Margarette**, my artist daughter; **Danver Jude**, my musically inclined and talented son; **Santino Miguel**, my engineer-in-the-making son; and **Christiann Mikhail**, my miracle boy. Mom loves you so much!

Thank you to my parents, **Nanay Yolly** and **Tatay Ver**, for your love and support; to my brothers, **Michael Angelo Vasquez** and **Marco Vasquez**. To my mother-in-law, **Virginia Santos**.

To all my students around the world, I thank you for inspiring me more to do what I need to do. I feel more blessed being connected with all of you.

Thank you, **Cora Cristobal**, founder of the Toronto Women's Club, for inspiring me to empower women.

A million thanks to this very special and humble human being, **Dr. John Gray**, who inspired me to write this book. He is the Bestselling Author of Men Are from Mars, Women Are from Venus. Thank you so much for taking the time to endorse MOMMY CAN BUY HAPPY NEST. I'll be forever grateful for the inspiration and support. God bless your generous heart.

And to all of you, my readers, I thank you for grabbing this book, especially to all the parents around the world. From my heart, I salute all of you. Kudos for a job well done!

Continue to be blessed and be a blessing to others.

Anna Santos
*Author, Speaker, Entrepreneur, and Life Coach*

# Mommy Can Buy Happy Nest

*3 Secrets to Having It All as A Woman*

# Anna Santos

MOMMY CAN BUY HAPPY NEST
*3 Secrets to Having It All as A Woman*

**www.annasantoshub.com**

Copyright © 2019 by ANNA SANTOS
ISBN: 978-1-77277-257-9

Limits of Liability and Disclaimer of Warranty

Warning – Disclaimer

Publisher
10-10-10 Publishing
Markham, ON
Canada
Printed in Canada and the United States of America

# TABLE OF CONTENTS

INTRODUCTION

# Men Are from Mars, Women Are from Venus

*"Men are motivated and empowered when they feel needed. Women are motivated and empowered when they feel cherished."*

– Dr. John Gray

IT'S BEEN SAID THAT THERE IS A COUNTLESS LIST OF DIFFERENCES between a man and a woman – the way they communicate, think, interpret things, and deal with their emotions, as well as their choices and preferences, priorities, and lifestyles.

Dr. John Gray, an American author and relationship counselor, wrote the book, *Men Are from Mars, Women Are from Venus*, back in the early 1990s and sold more than 50 million copies globally, according to CNN.

According to Dr. John Gray's observations, men and women speak differently in terms of tonality, verbiage, and delivery, affecting their ability to understand one another or react and respond to certain situations.

The main idea in his book talks about the truth that, if only the opposite sexes understand and embrace their respective differences, there will be much less friction and conflicts in their relationship and, for some, marriage.

He further stated that, "Men often complain; she is overreacting. And women complain, he doesn't listen."

I was inspired by Dr. Gray's viewpoints in his masterpiece, and I decided to mention some of them here in my Introduction, because in the following pages, I will focus more on every woman or mother to highlight her very interesting traits such that a man or a father can understand her more.

But hey, let me be clear. I'm not trying to be biased here. Yes, I'm a woman and a mother, and I can only speak as one and on behalf of our tribe in the world. Don't fret, gentlemen! Because I can modestly admit that sometimes, we, women, in fact, don't understand each other due to our hormonal changes, deep emotions, varying beliefs, different choices, cultural practices, core values, and so forth; everything is a big deal for us!

However, despite all these differences, I know that we were wonderfully and uniquely created with our distinct features and personalities – that our differences are not just normal, but are to be expected; that we are designed to be different in order to complement, as if we really came from different planets that gave justice to Dr. John Gray's creative interpretation that indeed men are from Mars, women are from Venus!

"When we look at the life stages of a woman, countless changes continue to happen in her body that only prove that these are a part of a massive preparation to the wonderful gift of motherhood."

# CHAPTER 1

# *Understanding A Woman*

*"Some men spend a lifetime in an attempt to comprehend the complexities of women. Others pre-occupy themselves with somewhat simpler tasks, such as understanding the theory of relativity."*
– Albert Einstein

## THE PHYSIOLOGY AND LIFE STAGES OF A WOMAN

**The Body**

In my Introduction, I have mentioned that a man and a woman are different in so many ways. And I want to get started with the very obvious – the body and its physiology.

I also mentioned that this book is more about a woman. Having that said, my focus will be on her.

She expresses her feelings differently from the way a man does—I will elaborate more on that later on.

I can tell from my own experience that, although a sudden burst of inexplainable feelings just comes out at no specific time of the day, there are triggering factors that can support such occurrence.

A woman's body is designed by our Divine Creator with the ability to bear a child in her womb for nine months, and amazing things happen inside it. Thanks to science that explains how this miracle happens for our better understanding.

It's also noteworthy, according to experts, that a woman's body is more tolerating to pain due to her tissue laxity, muscular flexibility, bone structures, and other supportive elements that develop during the grand hormonal shift of puberty in preparing her body for pregnancy.

In addition, a woman possesses more sexual organs both inside and outside her body, which I will not delve into much further. This made me start to understand even more the differences between my own body and my brothers' bodies by way of my father restricting me from doing activities he believed were unfit for a girl like me.

One day, I joined my brother in the backyard with his friend to ride a bike, only for my father to say that I couldn't. Without fully understanding the reason why, I had no choice but to follow his directive. I learned later on in life that it was because of the girl's hymen (a thin membrane that covers the external opening of a female's genital organ); my father believed that riding a bike can destroy it and can greatly affect my virginity – a very sacred possession in my culture.

Having four children, one girl and three boys, I have noticed that they don't really care about the activities they do and their limitations or restrictions that concern their body structures, unless made aware. I assumed that my brothers and I behaved the same way. We did not feel self-conscious about everything until our parents made us aware of it.

Because of this, we can all agree that a man and a woman are really different from each other in so many ways. But again, I'll focus more on a woman's distinctive attributes from inside out.

So, let's now move on to a woman's life stages.

## Puberty (Coming of Age)

Another prominent difference between a man and a woman is the stages of puberty that are more evident early on in a girl's body.

Puberty generally means the beginning years of adolescence in both sexes. They only differ in the manifestations such as the development of certain body organs, menstrual cycle (menarche), hormonal changes, voice changes, and hair growth, among others.

It is also worthy to note that puberty can occur either early or late, which experts say is primarily due to several factors such as inadequate nutrition, chronic illness, or severe levels of stress and problems associated with interactions between the brain and the reproductive system.

Apart from the physical changes happening in the coming of age for both genders, experts proved that psychological changes also occur. During this course of life, young people begin to shift away from concrete thinking to the more adult abstract way, which often represents the realities of life that include deciphering between good and bad, wrong and right, moral and immoral, ideologies and so forth.

I have asked fellow moms who happen to have both children of opposite sexes about their observations with regard to how a girl and a boy act, think, and communicate. Although I cannot clearly validate my hypothesis, I can only agree that they are really different in so many ways, so to speak.

Many of them say that girls think more maturely and display a greater sense of independence than boys do; also, girls are more responsible with regard to decision-making, household chores, and nurturing.

I have four children; two of them are teenagers, Sophia, a girl, aged 19; and Danver, a boy, aged 16.

We came to Canada in early 2006 as immigrants.

Sophia and Danver were only six and three years old at that time, respectively. Coming to a foreign country as a family with no extra help from other people in terms of childcare and supervision—especially when my husband and I would go to work—we would actually rely on Sophia's assistance at her young age to look after her younger sibling while I did some household chores.

Fast forward, my husband and I were gifted with two more children who were both born in Canada; Santino, aged 9; and Christiann, aged 5, at the time of this writing.

When Santino was born, Danver was seven years old. However, for some reason, I didn't feel quite comfortable leaving Santino under his care even for a short period of time. It might have been because of the opinions of other parents that influenced me, or maybe it was just embedded in my belief system that girls are naturally more compassionate because of that motherly instinct, regardless of age.

This may sound biased and hurt my son's feelings, but I cannot explain and elucidate the reasons behind it.

But let me tell you now that I'm neither a doctor nor an expert of some sort. Everything that I said here is based on my own personal life's experience, and some observations, research, and collaborations with other parents and moms. I do not intend to either validate or disprove ideas; my goal is to raise awareness about the differences between a man and a woman and how a father or a man can better understand a mom or a woman more for who she really is.

**Fertility**

Whether we like it or not, everyone is designed to naturally evolve to be able to take on greater responsibilities and opportunities for growth and development in this ever-changing world. A human being's evolution, for both man and woman, includes physiological changes that I mentioned above that occur in puberty and then to fertility stage.

For a girl, a fertility cycle starts with her menarche (or menstruation, as we all know) that usually comes monthly—every 28 days to most, but it may vary due to several factors such as hormonal imbalance, illnesses, biological age, and other factors.

Fluctuation in her mood is one of the effects of hormonal changes a woman undergoes as part of the fertility stage.

I don't know if this sounds weird, but I'd have a clue that my menstrual cycle is coming when I'd experience sudden cravings for salty foods and that vinegary taste. Without having to exactly know what date it is of the month, experiencing the said cravings will clearly remind me that my cycle is forthcoming.

I want to again stress the fact that I cannot delve into a man's fertility, not because I'm uninterested to talk about it, but because this book is primarily written to understand a woman from different perspectives—including her bodily functions—from inside out.

Experts have scientific explanations about the biological and chemical compositions of every woman's body, and I know that all of us women experience the same thing. As I've previously noted, we go through our life stages because our physical bodies are designed to co-create a precious life, which brings me down to the next subtopic: pregnancy.

**Pregnancy**

"What, for you, is the essence of being a woman?"

This was the exact question asked of a Miss Universe Pageant candidate from India, named Sushmita Sen, back in 1994. She won the title and was crowned Miss Universe at that time.

She answered by saying, "The origin of a child is a mother, and a mother is a woman who shares and shows the man what love, caring, and sharing is all about."

I was 18 years old at that time. Although, I couldn't totally appreciate her answer, it was embedded in my brain from that day up to this time. It had impacted me significantly, and I had come to really appreciate the value of motherhood.

Motherhood officially starts even before the child is born—from the time of conception. I know, and I'm sure that all mothers will agree with me when I say that there's no such thing as an easy pregnancy, let alone childbirth; however, it's just an amazing gift that a woman's body is able to perfectly respond to the power of co-creating and carrying a precious life in her womb.

When we look at the life stages of a woman, countless changes continue to happen in her body that only prove that these are a part of a massive preparation to the wonderful gift of motherhood.

Both physical and physiological changes in her body are even more prominent during and after pregnancy. Hair loss, sagging breasts and other parts of the body, stretch marks, broadening of the pelvic bones, and weakening of the teeth and bones are just a few changes that I personally experienced.

I must admit that I experience a mix of feelings each time I see a massive transformation in my physical body. I feel blessed and privileged to be a mom; however, in hindsight, I also feel unattractive and sometimes unwanted, which lowers my confidence and self-esteem.

Every mother I know feels the same way at some point in her life. And I think that it's normal. Feeling insecure or inferior becomes real, which again supports why a woman is sometimes hard to understand, especially from a man's perspective.

Although these changes are very obvious, I believe the difference lies in the way she should think about who she really is and what she is made of.

When I plainly think about childbirth, pain comes to my mind first—physical pain for the most part.

At one time, a friend asked me to realistically describe childbirth, on a pain scale of 1 to 10. And to be honest, it was just too easy for me to respond to my friend that no word can perfectly describe the pain associated with giving birth. In fact, 10, being the highest, is way too low to measure it.

But that question really made me think. So, I consulted my other friend, Mr. Google.

I found one answer online that childbirth is equivalent to twenty fractured bones altogether. Ouch! The word fracture alone is painful enough, for me. Imagine, 20 bones fracturing all at the same time? Really? On the other hand, reading through this interesting description— assuming it's true—I felt a sense of amazement. Amazed that I was able to bear twenty simultaneous fractured bones four times in my lifetime, giving birth to my four wonderful kids! Wow! Great job, Anna (I deserve a pat on my back).

But wait, there's more! A woman's incredible journey doesn't end there. From the coming of age to fertility stage, then to pregnancy (to most women), and—now here comes a remarkable part of the process—menopause. From the mouth of my own mother, I once heard her said this, "It's part of ageing. I'm menopausal."

## Menopause

And I asked her, "Mom, what? What is menopausal?"

Since I've not reached this stage yet, I've spoken to many women who are approaching menopause, as well as some who are already at this phase of their lives. I wanted to understand what it's like.

I'd also seen some prominent signs and changes in my mom's journey when she was at this stage.

My mother shared her own experiences when she reached her menopausal stage. She would have sudden outbursts of mood swings and irritability. In terms of physiological and bodily changes, she noticed some muscular pains and aches, headaches, bladder control issues, dryness in her femininity, and decreased sexual drive or libido.

She even mentioned feeling unworthy and depressed, which understandably had affected her emotional and intellectual wellbeing.

Science defines menopause as a normal condition in a woman's life that occurs typically between her early to mid-forties to about fifty years of age, whereby her menstrual cycle totally stops.

Still there are countless actions going on in a woman's body that make her male counterpart find it hard to really understand her. From the male perspective, women are just hard to comprehend. Period. And I don't blame them.

However, despite realizing how complicated a woman's physiology and her life stages are, I can speak for myself that I take pride in being a woman and how amazing it is to be one!

# DIFFERENT NEEDS

*"Then the Lord God made a woman from the rib He had taken out of the man, and He brought her to the man."*
– Gen. 2:22

From a religious point of view, God knew from the beginning of His creation of the entire universe that there are certain needs to be satisfied, especially for humans. When He created Adam (the first man in the history of creation in the book of Genesis), He decided to bring him his counterpart, named Eve (the first woman).

I'm not a Bible expert and I don't intend to make you believe what I believe and read, but for the purpose of a particular angle as to how humanity all started, it's been said that God, as the Creator of the universe, originally designed man (collective term used for both genders in the ancient times) to meet certain needs, which I will discuss in the following pages.

So, let's get started.

## Physical Need

I am a woman. I have different needs, including the physical. Through the sacrament of marriage (matrimony), my husband and I became one body. And going back to the teaching from the Holy Bible, the scriptural order of priorities should be spouse (after God), then children, parents, extended family, and then the rest of the world.

A woman is expressive of her feelings, both negative and positive.

I could remember when I had our fourth child. My sudden bliss of joy while holding my son, Christiann, in my arms was converted to feeling anxious, depressed, and exhausted from sleepless nights, let alone the physical pain from the stitches I had incurred through Caesarean section. I didn't know exactly what sort of position to make at that time, as every angle (standing up, sitting down, or lying in bed) seemed to be triggering the physical pain.

I felt so alone, misunderstood, and abandoned.

I'd initially perceived my husband, as he came home from work, to not care at all. Aside from a forehead kiss, which he normally would do, I needed more. I wished he'd sit beside me, offer his shoulder for my head to lean on, hug me, or talk to me.

More than sex, I needed gestures of affection and love—that I'm being cared for, too!

I felt I was depleting my love tank, running empty and in need of a refill.

I knew it would make a huge difference if we were having constant conversations; if he asked me questions such as, "How were things with you today?" Or "Have you eaten your lunch?" It may sound so plain to most people reading this book, but it is indeed special to me.

I'd proven it to be true that making my man guess what I wanted won't really work. Because he needed to be told. Seriously. And when conflicts would arise, he would know exactly what to do.

When my physical needs are met, it positively impacts my wellbeing, which then initiates a domino effect in everything in my life, in my loved ones' lives, and my environment.

I've learned that I am not the only one who'd complain about that sense of lack of empathy from a male partner, but most women I know would do, too!

Although "I love you" from my husband before and after work hours may sound routine every single day, I'd literally feel bad when he sometimes forgets to say it or to kiss me goodbye before he goes to work. I'd feel quite irritable the whole day.

As a wife, it is important that I feel pursued (not stalked) each time. Simple gestures such as massaging my feet, cooking my favorite dish, bringing home my favorite dessert, and the like make me remember our courtship stage. And it really makes me happy.

Generally speaking, every woman I know naturally

needs a form of declaration that she is loved in any way possible, be it physical or emotional, which I will be talking about next.

## Emotional Need

When a woman reaches adolescence or the age of consent to enter a romantic relationship with the opposite sex until marriage, she tends to long for a very strong need to satisfy her emotions.

Because every woman I know believes that physical demonstrations of affection are not enough for her, she still needs more validation that touches her feelings. A man's emotions can be relayed to a woman without words, using the touch of his hand, or by giving her flowers. Spending some time with her, listening to her concerns, helping with the household chores, and a million more little things will surely make her the happiest woman in the world.

I can tell from my own experience that shopping is not my husband's cup of tea, but when I'd ask him to go with me to shop, he'd agree to go with me, even though he knew he'd feel bored. It would just make me giggle on the inside when I'd see him find ways to kill boredom. I really appreciated his gesture.

That's affection to me.

Another way to satisfy a woman's emotional need is by our male partner's demonstration of honesty and openness. What becomes the most common cause of partners' conflict is the issue of trust, especially when actions don't match the words. One specific example is when saying "I love you." A woman can feel whether it's just out of obligation as a partner or a sincere expression of love.

There are still much more that I'd like to include in the list, and talking about this need may cover the entire chapter.

In essence, understanding a woman with regard to her emotions and feelings can lift up her morale in so many ways.

Her emotional need can also be filled by other sources such as family and friends, which I will discuss more in the next need: social need.

## Social Need

"No man is an island." The word "man" here doesn't literally mean just our opposite sex; it's just a collective term for both genders.

This tagline means that nobody is self-sufficient and that everyone relies on others. Every human being needs to be a part of a community in order to thrive and grow.

I may not be 100 percent correct, but based on my observation, women are more interested in socializing, seeking friendships, connections, and communicating with others.

I am more of a conversationalist than my husband. I

love talking to people, listening to their stories, and sharing mine as well.  I love going to social events, meeting new friends, and expanding my network.

Women, they say, are naturally the talkers, as they love to start the conversation most of the time.  Although this may not always apply, I partly agree with it.  Women always find the door to enter a conversation.

When I used to be employed and would take the public transport to and from work, I was able to connect with many people by talking to them, so much so that I would often end up almost missing my station.  I think I have mastered the art of opening a conversation by simply looking for something to talk about like the weather conditions for the day, the nice purse or the jacket, and current events.

Talking to people makes me happy.

Attention and appreciation of my presence matter to me much.

Friendships and healthy social wellbeing also make me the happiest.

I also find joy as a woman from engaging in social groups to empower and lead, knowing that I have the voice to be heard and that my opinion matters.

Although I'm married, individuality as a woman is also important to me.  There are some instances where I'd prefer to be around like-minded women with the same core values, beliefs, and goals in life.

To my husband, I'd always feel the need to play the role as a wife. I'm trusted to run the household, from raising our children, to independently making some decisions that don't need further deliberation, handling our finances, and much more. I also have the need to be heard when I'm excited or frustrated. I need healthy relationships, and these give me more meaning in life.

**Personal Need**

When I was still single with no responsibilities and obligations other than myself, I've had all the freedom to do whatever I wanted. I didn't have to ask for anybody's permission or wait for approval for every decision I'd make, from smallest to biggest. It has been much different since I've been married, because I'm not on my own and my decisions affect the family.

Buying my personal stuff, for instance, was merely part of my routine when I was not married and had no children yet. And every woman I know had that sense of vanity at some point in her life, especially during her younger years. However, I noticed that the majority of moms I met, myself included, lost their interest in even applying lipstick.

I can honestly say from my very own experience that, after giving birth, I lost my self-confidence. I felt unattractive, unwanted. And talking to moms with the same sentiments made this feeling even worse.

I even felt unappreciated. Not needed. Unworthy.

Because of that sense of unworthiness, I began to lose interest in going to a salon for my hair, for my foot spa, or massage.

I felt I was a totally different person from years back.

It was when depression and anxiety attacks set in. What made me go back to the original "self" was the change of heart, realizing that I need to serve and love myself first such that I can offer more and give more.

The emptiness I felt inside me was filled by looking after what I personally needed first. I needed to be "me" — the real me.

## Financial Need

They say that men want beauty and women want financial security from relationships.

This popular dogma is being portrayed in movies, soap operas, and even in books that most women want rich men, and men want beautiful and sexy women.

I am not in the position to validate this, but if I may share my personal opinion, I'd be a hypocrite if I wouldn't prefer a guy with a steady income, at least. And I think this criterion of financial security with regard to choosing a life partner or a man to marry is more obvious as a woman matures. I must admit, in my younger years, physical attributes were more important to me.

What typical parents would wish for their daughter

to marry is the ability of the man to, not only love her, but financially support her and their future children.

Ethnicity and culture also play a role when talking about satisfying a woman's financial needs.

I know of a cultural practice whereby the wife and the husband don't mix their finances together, having their respective bank accounts. And I wonder how financially secure a wife feels if the husband's money is only his or if the wife cannot access his funds. Although I cannot judge that practice, I personally may feel financially insecure, especially in my case that I am a stay-at-home mom and not earning a steady income.

With regard to how a couple manages their finances, having one household bank account or at least having mutual access to the funds regardless of who pays for what, works better.

I also find it easier to track where every penny goes when there's autonomy in financial management of a household.

At some point in our marriage, my husband and I would take turns handling our overall budget. Although we have different bank accounts, both of us can access them at any given time.

Also, when funds are consolidated, it's much easier to save money due to proper allocation of expenses.

A woman needs to be financially secured. And here are a few reasons why: 1) She has many people to take care of, including her children, ageing parents, needy extended family members and friends. 2) She usually runs the numbers for budgeting at home. 3) She lives longer (in most cases) than her spouse. 4) She feels more equipped to know that she has a tool to use for growth; and 5) She feels more at peace, knowing that she's covered.

# MYSTERIES OF A WOMAN

*"Women. They are a complete mystery."*
– Stephen Hawking

Understanding a woman is just like solving a puzzle. It can never be considered complete when there are still some pieces missing.

While there are obvious physiological reasons that contribute to a woman's outlandish behaviors most of the time, understanding her fully requires more familiarity of her inner core, which makes her mysterious in the first place.

### Internal Monologue and Self-Talk

Don't be scared of me because I have to confess something.

Do you know that I would sometimes catch myself engaging in my own internal monologue and self-talk, without even consciously knowing that I'm actually doing it? In fact, I asked some of my friends, especially women, if they do the same.

Here you go! I just squealed one of a woman's mysteries. I'm actually getting some validation from others, as this gives me that sense of relief that I'm not insane or something.

Why self-talk?

Being a full-time mom to my four amazing children and a wife to my wonderful husband, while running my businesses at home, I have so many things going on in my brain on a consistent basis. I can sometimes actually hear a soft voice in my head. Thoughts can range from small to big things that may relate to random occurrences, plans, or just bizarre ideas. That inner, soft voice provides a running monologue at some point during the day. Although it entertains my doubts and fears, I'd suddenly shift gears to bolster my positive thoughts, relating to my goals and dreams.

I use my self-talk to challenge and destroy that negative critic in me, and then build back my self-confidence.

Again, based on my personal experience and observation, self-talk is more common in women. That internal monologue goes on and on and on, only to suddenly realize that our brain waves are flying to the ether.

Sometimes when I feel unheard, my first impulse

would be to talk to myself. And I realized that self-talk reduces my stress levels.

When one of my kids would get sick, not knowing what to do, I'd suddenly hear myself talking. Then, suddenly, I'd know what to do next.

I also find that my internal monologue can motivate me. When I would start to open my mouth and whisper words as if there's a real conversation happening with another person, ideas and inspirations would come to my thoughts. Vivid images would come across my mind, leaving me excited inside.

When I want to address a sensitive issue with my husband and I sense that something just seemed a little off, I'd start to indulge in self-talk to prepare myself for a more serious one-on-one conversation. I'd have the opportunity to practice empathy by talking to myself, and putting my husband's proverbial shoe on my foot. Because of that, more often than not, we would end up resolving our issues amicably.

## Between the Lines

I didn't require him to be a genius. I just want him to understand me between the lines!

He sometimes gets on my nerves, seriously.

When I'd spell out the word, W-O-R-L-D, and I'd ask you now to write it down on a piece of clean paper, I'd conclude that the only thing you'd see is the word, WORLD.

Right? Good. It's neat, clear, and very straightforward.

However, I believe, it becomes quite different when wives talk to their husbands or partners, for instance. More often than not, what women say in words in fact mean something else that are intended to be understood by men, with that expectation that they understand it.

"Hon, I'm tired. What a long day today. My body hurts. I don't feel like moving around."

Yes, the sentences are in plain English. No jargons whatsoever. And I want him to get the message.

I want him to do something for me. I want him to offer me a cup of tea, a foot massage, whatever it is.

Without being told, I just want him to do something about it! And read or understand between the lines.

It really annoys me if he doesn't get that. And how do I know that he doesn't actually get it?

Well, I'd know that he's not "mentally" there with me when he won't even ask me questions like, "Do you want me to massage you?" OR "What can I do to make you feel better?"

Ladies, are you with me?

There can also be instances where an absolute silence on my part means something else. When I'm not in the mood, I'd usually just remain quiet the whole time, albeit my husband knows it's not my nature. When I'm in my normal state of sanity, I'd talk more than anybody else around the house. When feelings of severe irritability and anger attack me, I'd also choose to be silent and not say a thing at all because I don't want to regret it after saying hurtful words, and it can also give me the opportunity to reflect about the incident.

However, this drives him crazy at times. When I'm being asked about what's wrong, I'd say, "Nothing is wrong." Then, of course, as a normal human being would do, he'd stop asking more, and that pisses me off. Crazy as it sounds, I actually wanted him to ask me more until he learns that I'm not okay!

Women are very good at paying attention to details. Because of that, we expect men to follow the same. However, it has been one of the common aspects that they don't understand in us women.

## It's Not Just Red

For women, saying red to a color is not enough. What men know is that it's one of the primary colors and that's it! For them, red is red. But we know that it has tons of varying shades like crimson, burgundy, scarlet, cherry, brick, rosewood, raspberry, carmine, and others.

Friday nights are our date nights every single week. While it's supposed to be a time for relaxation and getting away from the noise of the world and the monotonous daily routines, it usually would create some friction when deciding what type of food to eat. When he'd ask me where I wanted to eat, I'd say, "Wherever you want." And when he'd suggest a place, I'd say, "Why there?" When a place was finally agreeable to me, he'd ask then what I'd like to eat. I'd say, "Anything would be good for me." However, when a menu he'd suggest wouldn't suit my taste, I'd suddenly feel irritable.

I know, it's weird. He'd say, "Woman, make up your mind! Are you playing games with me?"

In hindsight, it's crazy. I know!

Again, ladies, are you with me?

There was a study that a woman's brain has different boxes. There's a box for everything. It was also described that a woman's brain is made up of a huge ball of wire and that every single strand of it is connected to everything, which now looks like an intermingled wire, so to speak.

Experts say that there are brain differences between the two genders, including the cognitive and processing aspects, structural differences, chemical composition, hormones, blood flow, and brain activities, to name a few.

And there are certain things that every man should also understand about a woman's brain. If that happens, it is less likely that misinterpretation of implied actions can be avoided. However, in fairness to every man, we, women, should also understand the male brain.

Most women change every day based on their cycles and hormonal changes in their bodies. It's one of our body's response mechanisms that will automatically come every single month. We also think intuitively, and

I'll discuss more about it in the following pages.

I hate every conflict, but lack of response triggers me to hate it even more, especially from my husband. I expect him to read my mind. There are definitely much more in a woman's brain.

I love to use my intuition rather than facts. I'm likely to use my emotions more than rationale. I require more details than generalized information. I want to be understood, rather than offered solutions.

And this is how my brain works.

# STRENGTHS AND WEAKNESSES

*"A strong woman accepts both compliments and criticisms graciously, knowing that it takes both sunshine and rain for a flower to grow."*
– Mandy Hale

There's no point in comparing the physical strengths of a man and a woman due to the inherent differences in their body structures, compositions, and purposes.

A man is expected to do labour or heavier manual jobs because his build can handle them well. A woman's body is designed to carry a baby, and her flexibility related to that causes all the wonders for that purpose.

Strengths and weaknesses are not just about

the physical capabilities, but more about the intrinsic characteristics that make a man and a woman totally different.

One of my favorite songs in the 1980s, "Boys Don't Cry," was popularized by an American rock band, The Cure. And the Chorus goes:

"I tried to laugh about it, cover it all up with lies
I tried to laugh about it, hiding the tears in my eyes
'Coz boys don't cry...Boys don't cry."

When my mom would reprimand my older brother for the silly things he did and he'd be in the verge of crying, she would suddenly say, "I don't want to hear you crying. Boys don't cry."

During my younger years, I had circle of friends, both boys and girls. There was a huge difference in the way they handled heartbreaks from romantic relationships.

I'd easily cry. My girl friends would also do the same. But boys were totally different, as if nothing happened to them—at least on the surface.

Why am I saying this?

According to most men I know, crying is a sign weakness. And that could be the reason why we seldom see them crying. The belief that crying is not for boys is continuously embedded in our society. But why?

We know that women easily cry, regardless if it's

tears of joy or otherwise. Simple triggers make us cry.

Experts say that crying is not a demonstration of weakness, but rather of strength. It's our natural response to certain stimuli as our way to cope and process situations.

But I cannot absolutely judge that boys who don't cry are weak while girls who cry are strong. My whole point is that women easily respond to the body's mechanisms, and they are noted to be, in fact, emotionally strong. Women demonstrate emotions right away—every single bit of it— and crying is one of them.

On the other hand, a woman's weakness always relates to something that touches her emotions and anything that she values the most. You can easily move a woman and bring her to both joy and sorrow when a button is pushed to trigger them.

During the primitive years, women were confined to homes only and not allowed to be involved in civic and social gatherings, political spectrum, and even in businesses. In that sense, women had no voice and were never allowed to participate.

In today's generation, women are encouraged to go out and take part in every single arena. We now have equal opportunities as the opposite sex. We now have a voice, and it signifies strength; empowered women, as they call us now.

Women are now free to lead and speak, as we see female leaders in our society.

As for me, my strengths and weaknesses are directly linked to my relationships with my family, friends, business partners, churchmates, and every person I meet every single day.

## THE SIXTH SENSE

*"Never underestimate the power of a woman's intuition. Some women can recognize a game before you even play it."*
– Unknown

Generally, men wonder how their partners (girlfriends or wives) are able to detect dishonesty or other acts of unfaithfulness, as if they're being spied on. They've been sold by the belief that all women possess an extra power, their sixth sense, also called intuitive power or simply intuition.

Our five fundamental senses include sight, smell, taste, hearing, and touch. Intuition may also be called Extrasensory Perception or ESP, being referred to as the sixth sense.

But why is intuition often mostly attached to women and not in men?

Some say that intuition is developed in women due to the cultural expectations placed on them, as they're being groomed to raise children, which then leads to the development of stronger instincts out of necessity. Also, women are known to be overly attached to their feelings—thus being emotional around things—while men are noted to be rational. Women often follow their gut feeling, especially in making decisions and judging situations, even without any precise evidence.

According to experts, women's sixth sense or intuition can be easily explained by our tendency to have a better use of the right side of our brain, which is more associated with the intuitive perception. And, of course, we are more in touch with our emotions and feelings, which allows us to be more intuitive.

We have the ability to sense the unknown even without being told, especially by mere observations.

One of the best pieces of advice my late grandmother gave me was to never spend my second thoughts on something, especially when my gut feeling doesn't agree with it.

It was a Saturday morning when one of my university friends called me to invite me to an unplanned field trip. I agreed to come, immediately packed my things, and proceeded to our meeting place. However, when our service car was about to start driving, I felt something different inside me and told the driver to open the car. While my friends were yelling behind and asking why, I ignored the noise and immediately got off, saying, "I changed my mind."

Hours later, I received a phone call that the car had

crashed, injuring several of the people inside the car. Fortunately, nobody died, except for a life-threatening injury in one of the passengers. What was supposed to be an enjoyable trip turned out to be a traumatic experience for everyone. Although I still believed in fate, had I not listened to my grandmother's advice, I would be part of that nightmare.

The said event not only became a huge lesson for me, but also strengthened my belief in the power of gut feeling or intuition. I still follow my grandmother's advice up to this point, especially when I feel something is not right.

It also proves that when we make use of our intuition, we are more likely to benefit from it, as it provides deeper understanding and judgment without any rational justification or analytical thinking. But I have to make my personal disclaimer here that not every gut feeling is accurate. My point is that, if it feels right, then go for it. We may, of course, still use our intellect in certain situations, especially when it's too obvious to do so.

What actually helped me to trust my intuition in the first place is to be mindful of what's really going on and then connect it to my inner core such as my feelings and my innate ability to decipher between right and wrong, or simply what feels right for me. In the process, I'd say that when that inner voice tries itself to be heard, then it might be really appropriate to listen to that voice. And that's how I use my sixth sense to my advantage.

Using my intuition as a mother also benefited my family most of the time. Mothering four children, I must admit that there were times when I'd overlook their needs. However, I'd know something was wrong right away when my eyes were set on one of them. With just a glance, I knew that my attention was needed to get it fixed. There were countless instances when my intuition or gut feeling saved our family from experiencing big troubles.

Thank God, I'm a woman!

# CHAPTER 2

# Defining Quality of Life

*"Life is what happens to you while you're busy making other plans."*

– John Lennon

WHAT IS QUALITY OF LIFE OR QOL?

According to Wikipedia, quality of life is the general wellbeing of individuals and societies, outlining negative and positive features of life. It observes life satisfaction, including everything from physical health, family, education, employment, wealth, safety and security to freedom, religious beliefs, and the environment. It should not be confused with the concept of standard of living, which is based primarily on income.

According to Encyclopaedia Britannica, it is the degree to which an individual is healthy, comfortable, and able to participate in or enjoy life events. The term *Quality of Life* is inherently ambiguous, as it can refer both to the experience an individual has of his or her own life, and to the living conditions in which individuals find themselves.

According to my own definition, quality of life is finding that absolute balance between my life's priorities (my healthy relationships) and other things that I love to do, either as a business or just merely a passion, that give me peace of mind, joy, and a sense of fulfillment—things that money can't buy.

If you come to think of it, defining quality of life can be subjective, because everyone is different. Some may base it on money and material possessions, while others may see it as a healthy state of his/her wellbeing that brings him/her happiness and fulfillment.

What about you? What's quality of life for you?

## Life Before the Commitment and Responsibilities

My definition of quality of life changed when I married my husband and became a mom to my four wonderful kids. Everything has to fit in with my family's welfare and wellbeing first before myself. Every time I see them happy, I feel the happiest.

I used to not worry too much about anything when I was still single, wild, and free. I carried no obligations whatsoever. There's nothing to think about but my next adventures after each paycheck.

But, really, who are we as a woman? Why were we created after men? And how would the world look like without us, women?

You can pause here and ponder for a second.

A woman plays different roles, which makes this world a better and a colorful place to live in. Would you agree?

Before she is someone else, she is a daughter first. I, myself, am a daughter—in fact, the only daughter, alongside my two older brothers. And I have to say that a part of my life is defined by my role as a daughter to my beloved parents. However, that God-given role, since birth, has defined what and who I'm supposed to be, and I let that role become me and rule over me.

My mother was very hands-on in terms of raising us, her children. And she taught us how to be responsible around the house by doing some light chores. However, I noticed a difference in the nature of the tasks given to me and my other brother. To sweep the floor was not my brother's task, but mine. Washing the dishes and clothes were not his either. Why was there a restriction? I knew we were both capable of doing such tasks. But why?

Until one day, I was feeling sick and couldn't do my assigned chores. Dirty dishes were lying in the sink unwashed. My older brother was there, doing nothing.

My mother, on the other hand, took the initiative to do it on my behalf, saying, "It's not for boys to do."

When I began to reach my adolescent stage, with the same chore assignments in my household, my mother said that I should start learning to cook more dishes to feed my family one day, and to be appreciated by my future mother-in-law.

You see, I felt I was brought up being defined—according to my roles as a good daughter and a good sister—then soon thereafter being a good wife, a good daughter-in-law, and a good mother. We are constantly defined, and every definition seems to never stop.

And because I'm a girl, I was made to believe that I should act like one; I was expected to play roles attached to my gender, and meet the expectations laid upon me.

What about this? Is there such a thing as a good woman? Or a good wife in marriage?

## Marriage

As my mother instilled in me the idea of the possible roles I'd play, such as being a wife and a mom, my father, on the other hand, reminded my unmarried brother that a massive preparation is needed for him to become the primary provider for the family.

That's one of the few things I could remember in our random conversation as a family.

However, I believe that, with tons of expectations laid upon us, including our readiness to take care of our spouses, run the household, and fulfill the duties that go with motherhood and parenting, it may be prudent that every woman in the world wanting to enter marriage, should take a training program, if at all possible. It's just me. No overstatement intended.

So, how does the quality of life look like for a typical woman, becoming a wife?

"Your wedding day is one of the most important days of your life," reads a line from a blog post online.

I'm happily married to my wonderful husband, Chris. While being single and obligation-free was far beyond compare to being a wife to Chris, I'd still choose the latter.

Quality of life in marriage is not a bed of roses, generally speaking. The "live happily ever after" notion doesn't really exist. Walt Disney movies are a good source to demonstrate how it's like, and fictitious stories in our libraries illustrate this perfectly.

But what really exists, I believe, is the "happy wife, happy life" notion. And it's one quality of life I appreciate in mine.

Being happy doesn't literally mean the absence of sadness, chaos, woes, and all that inside marriage. But one must know — especially the unmarried — that it is these challenges that add color to the bond. Most of the time, it is in the reconciliation after arguments that make the connection between the husband and wife stronger, when every confrontation turned into a victory, regardless of who throws the towel in first.

An effective communication between a husband and a wife in such a manner that one is willing to listen or give is also a good quality of life.

I've spoken to a relationship coach who has been happily married for almost four decades now, and I asked if he believes in the motto "Happy Wife, Happy Life." He said he doesn't, but rather he believes in making their lives together happy, thus making his wife happy.

Another relationship coach said that marriage is not a 50/50 partnership but rather 100/100, which means that a partner doesn't only give 50 percent of himself or herself to make up the 100, as they are both required to give their 100 percent to have a happy and long-lasting relationship.

Aside from communication, spending quality time together is another powerful ingredient to provide a very good quality of life for couples.

There's a massive list of things needed to make a marriage work successfully.

Decision-making is also part of providing a harmonious quality of life in marriage. This doesn't only include major purchases such as homebuying, career change, and so on. I've met some couples who found it quite difficult to decide, and this sometimes creates conflicts when choosing quality of life between having a child and a childless relationship. But I have to make a disclaimer that being childless doesn't really apply to every couple, as it's not always by choice; factors such as fertility and health issues, finances, cultural and religious practices sometimes play a role.

Either way, whatever the case may be, the quality of life depends on how a couple in a relationship defines it. People are different, with varying preferences, cultural practices, values, and upbringings.

And whether a couple chooses to have children or not, I believe that all women have that motherly instinct, which brings me to my second topic: Motherhood and Parenting.

## Motherhood and Parenting

I am a mother to my four children: two teenagers and two toddlers. Both age groups need my full attention. Mothering them requires more of my strength because of four different and interesting personalities. My role to them as a mom makes me someone with super powers; not like those of the superheroes we see in movies, but rather the abilities to transform myself to the person each of my children requires because of their uniqueness.

Let me go back to Chapter 1 where I wrote:

"What, for you, is the essence of being a woman?"

Without digging more into what's really obvious, without women, the human race would cease to exist.

A woman carries a child in her womb for nine months and then gives birth to a new life. Most mothers are physically there for their child(ren) to support, witness, and experience every milestone. She is the superwoman who performs every role she can to the best of her abilities.

When does a woman actually become a mother? What an interesting question!

Is it in the moment of conception? The plus sign on the pregnancy test? Or the positive result from a blood work at the doctor's office?

Motherhood is, for me, a decision and a state of mind. Some women I know have no children, but they play the role of a mother to someone else's child. How is it possible?

An aunt, a friend, a sister, whoever. Anybody can be a mother to anybody. There are no set-in-stone qualifications to becoming a mother. Mothering is also known as nurturing and loving another person, with physical demonstration of such.

I can only speak for myself about what motherhood to my four beautiful children is like inside my household.

Motherhood is one of the most difficult jobs there is. It basically marks a whole new chapter in a woman's life stage and story. It creates that power, the power that I've previously mentioned, which is something you actually didn't know was there until you had children. Mothering, they say, is using a woman's every emotion most of the time.

Now, parenting; is it different from mothering?

Mothering and parenting are interconnected in so many ways, but experts say that they are not exactly the same; the former is distinct to the individual—touching more on the emotional aspect—while parenting is more likely fuelled by academics and standards set by childcare experts. Almost all mothers I know use their motherly instincts and compassion for their children, while sometimes affected or influenced by the overabundance of advices from fellow moms or from what we call self-styled experts.

We were not born mothers; we become mothers. There was no manual given as to how we operate or get started. We figure things out in the process. We discover new things every single day.

Being a mom or a parent, running the household, is tough. And there are two sides I discovered when performing this role.

When I had my first child, there was this sense of unexplainable feeling, a spontaneous feeling of bliss when I heard my baby girl cry. Sophia was my firstborn. My whole world felt differently from the inside out. I had a precious, physically fragile life in my arms, which I'd promised to take care of and love with all my strength all the days of my life.

Motherhood gave me that sense of a beautiful purpose and a deeper meaning in life, not just to one child but four in my lifetime as a woman. That's the exciting side.

Compassion as a person—not just as a mom—especially to someone who's not able to independently take care of oneself, kicks in. And this noble role requires much work. Much sacrifice. Much understanding. Much of you!

From a biological mother's standpoint, pregnancy becomes the start of the tough journey. With all these physical, hormonal, emotional, social changes, and other variations in a woman's wellbeing—I can tell you from my own experience that it's not easy. Many of you can relate with me, too!

So, what's on the other side?

There are countless changes in a woman; pregnancy hormones cause unpredictable mood swings and irritability, easy fatigability, and much, much more.

After the child is born, there's a huge impact on her lifestyle due to sleep deprivation, changes in the priority matrix, major decisions based on finances, and so on. Her relationships with other household members such as her spouse or life partner and other children at home are also affected. Among others, her ability to free up some time for herself—such as leisure and "me" time—is almost out of the equation.

Because women are mostly expected to play the major role in running the household and raising the children, sharing responsibilities becomes an untouched topic between couples—married or unmarried—who have children.

Shared parenting is viewed as beneficial to both parents and children, encouraging to uplift the morale of all parties involved. Good relationships among members become the most obvious result of sharing responsibilities in raising the children and completing the housework. When both parents are hands-on, both are enabled to learn and grow together, thus creating that solid source of love and affection to give to their children and other dependents. Thus, improving the quality of life for all.

Mothering and/or parenting provides that sense of actually giving a portion of our life to manifest our love as a mother or as a dad, but it doesn't have to be the cause of losing our own lives just because we can only give what we have.

Shared parenting doesn't literally always mean equal distribution of work between mom and dad. Every couple differs, according to needs and lifestyle. There's no right or wrong, I suppose. So long that it's been agreed upon by both parties, it's good.

Because the truth of the matter is, whatever works for you is the best you should follow and do.

## Two Shifts

Working from 8 to 4 or 9 to 5 is the typical eight-hour work shift in the corporate world. We call it a day job. But being a mother and a wife—whether she's employed or not—shifts can be around the clock. She's always on-call—worse than a medical doctor!

And I want to emphasize on how a woman can perform two roles in two shifts.

Let's get started.

### Work and/or Career vs. Stay-At-Home Mom

As a woman who runs a household and then works for money, I require two shifts.

I'm a mom and a wife first, which I had described above—thus making up my first shift. And then everything that goes after that role, becomes my second shift.

I used to be employed as part of the corporate world for roughly two decades, working for a boss in a typical office setting, where my eight-hour-plus days were spent five days a week.

Being in the medical field required full attention and time, because we deal with the lives of our patients. Requesting a vacation was not always an option for me for two important reasons: First, my department needed me because I had no reliever to do the job in my absence. Second, I couldn't afford to have a cut in my paycheck, especially when my vacation leave had run out, or it would be financial chaos for my family.

My job felt so monotonous to me, as I would do just the same things over and over again every single day.

But it wasn't actually my real problem.

I never had the chance to volunteer or even show up to my kids' activities in school. Not even witnessing my children receive their awards. How painful was that? Not only had I denied them my presence when they needed me, but I could not also provide them with well-prepared meals, which would have left me with no option but to buy them commercially prepared snacks instead, because I didn't have time to cook.

With all these things reaching over and above the roof, how could I even possibly have time to look after my own self or have that chance to think about what I loved to do or pursuing my passion and dreams?

Until I made one of the toughest, but most rewarding, decisions in my life.

From being a corporate employee and a career-oriented woman, I shifted my gear to...

Being a Stay-At-Home Mom, officially!

And here's one example of the quality of life for a stay-at-home mom, just like yours truly, including the challenges and the wins.

There is quite a good number of challenges in being a stay-at-home mom. Apart from the financial side, moms who took that plunge to be more domesticated are being judged by other people and even by fellow moms themselves, regarding many things. With overabundance of advices from here and there, the quality of life becomes too confusing due to the validity of many decisions being made.

After giving birth to my fourth child and undergoing post-partum depression, I had decided to leave my corporate job and be an official stay-at-home mom in August of 2016. From the perspective of a careerwoman whose level of comfort in the corporate setting is fairly high, it was next to impossible to just leave the environment where I had spent my life of over two decades, doing the things at which I was an expert. It was a challenge that, although I may have some ideas to get started with a business to support my husband, I was really afraid of the unknown. Too many things were bothering my whole being as to whether resigning from work was the best decision to make.

I'm grateful that my decision turned out to be not just good, but the best!

It's more akin to winning the lottery, indeed.

I never liked being in the kitchen in the past. You know why? Because I could not manage it! I had so much to deal with, that it became my least priority. And there was this guilt feeling of not being able to prepare my family home-cooked food. As a mom, it is one of the most painful feelings.

But this time around, kitchen is my happiness and a place for my expression of love to them. Providing them now with their favorite dishes, makes me feel more fulfilled as a mom and a wife; sharing food and stories on the kitchen table is one of our best bonding moments. Their words of appreciation are music to my ears, and the smiles on their faces are like a masterpiece artwork. It's priceless!

Then, after the kids have gone to school and my husband to work, I can enjoy my "me" time however I want it spent—be it for my connection with God and nature, self-development, or, of course, my several businesses that now provide more income streams than my past employment.

I am now able to attend to my kids' awarding ceremonies at school where I can freely take photos and video-record the precious moments. For me, it's more than winning the lottery, I guess! On top of that, I enjoy being a parent volunteer in their excursions. I love it when my kids feel so proud to tell their classmates that they have their mom on board. Isn't it cool? It's cool, for them, as it is for me.

Choosing to transition from commute to telecommute as a stay-at-home mom benefited my husband and children, and all the more myself.

Due to my flexible hours, I can choose to work as I please and select the people I want to work with.

CHAPTER 3

# Secret One Revealed : Self-Mastery

*"Knowing yourself is the beginning of all wisdom."*
– Aristotle

WE WERE ALL BORN NAKED AND NOT KNOWING ANY SINGLE thing. From that level, everyone starts out just the same. I believe that everything we acquire—be it knowledge, values, or beliefs—each and every single day is fairly contributed by the environment in which we belong, including our family, friends, classmates, co-workers; the list goes on and on.

I used to have that strong desire to be a medical doctor since I was five years old; I can't exactly remember how my aspiration started. However, I recall one impactful comment by my late maternal grandmother about my social skills. She said that, because I loved talking to people, telling stories about anything, and communicating with them at the age of three, I would be a good fit to becoming a medical doctor and helping others.

I asked people from different age groups how they had come up with a dream to pursue when they grow up. Some of them said from their parents' expectations, some said it was because of peer pressure, and some chose those paths merely because it was the trend, while others were uncertain.

Becoming who we are in the process is the sum total of our daily encounters with our own selves and the outside world we live in that then affects how we regard ourselves as; thus, making it quite vague to define who we really are or being aware of what we innately have. Self-mastery brings out that power to know and discover more about you!

So, what really is SELF-MASTERY?

According to Wiktionary, self-mastery is the conscious control of one's behaviour.

I am inspired by this famous quote:

*"Watch your thoughts, for they become words.*
*Watch your words, for they become actions.*
*Watch your actions, for they become habits.*
*Watch your habits, for they become character.*
*Watch your character, for it becomes your destiny."*

There are certain elements to a successful self-mastery. I will discuss them one by one.

And here it goes...

## Self-Concept

It all begins with looking in the mirror, asking yourself, "Who are you?", "What makes you YOU?" Or "What are you made of?"

From the way we were brought up by our parents, coupled with several factors such as environment and cultural practices, we have built a bundle of beliefs about ourselves and our lives.

We all started with zero self-concept, as it only develops as time passes by and life experiences happen in our lives.

According to Brian Tracy, a well-known leadership and motivational speaker about self-development, self-concept is our master program. In other words, it is what we think we are.

Experts also say that self is perhaps the most complex subject to study in psychology, just because of different preferences, lifestyle, and personality traits and beliefs that are quite hard to understand. Everyone's behavior may differ due to the factors I have mentioned above. Self-concept is believed to be of utmost importance in knowing about our self-perceptions and why we exist.

Sigmund Freud, an Austrian neurologist and founder of psychoanalysis, popularized a psychoanalytic theory that talks about the unconscious motives that control human behaviours.

It was noted that self-concept is learned—meaning, it can be developed as a person grows and ages. Our perceptions about who we are and how we see ourselves can be moulded and shaped—and even altered—just because of the significant factors around us.

Self-concept is indeed the end result of being able to immerse ourselves in the world. However, self-concept may not always agree with how others treat you. For example, I know I'm a very approachable person and I'm easy to get along with, but others may see me as strict and reserved.

My perception about "me" when I haven't discovered and immersed myself in self-mastery to discover more about who I really am is very far from what I know now. I used to be enclosed by my many self-limiting beliefs, caused by my own failures that I measured in congruence with the thoughts that I am limited, I am not capable, and I am not good enough.

I have observed that people who have mastered themselves can change the dynamics of their self-concept, leaving their old belief system behind, and instead afforded them to amplify their abilities to do wonderful things and appraise themselves with whom they really are. This becomes evident when a person says, "I'm better than I was yesterday."

## Self-Identity

Self-identity is not particularly evident until a person is exposed to more experiences that bring out who he/she really is.

You imagine yourself back in grade school when everything seemed to be generic.

When a child starts to show a special or an above-average trait, especially in the first few years in school, be it in academics, sports, or extra curricular activities, he/she is identified as somebody who is likely to succeed in the field associated with that trait.

Self-identity becomes quite complex, particularly when one is asked "Who are you?" Does it necessarily mean that you identify yourself according to your group affiliations or associations, your job, your religion, culture, and other factors?

What makes you different from others?

Because of our continuous social interactions among our peers in this world that we live in, there is a call to distinguish ourselves from others, which in that sense creates a comparison with other people and thus also builds social standards.

I am a mother to two teenagers, ages 19 and 16, at the time of this writing.

As we are now in the digital age, I can honestly say that I was raised differently by my parents as compared to how I raise my children these days.

I didn't actually know that there was such a thing as self-identity. All I knew was I needed to follow what my parents would tell me, what time I'd go home from school, what types of friends I'd hang out with, what clothes I should wear, and so on.

Self-identity was totally an unfamiliar term for me. However, when I became a mom of a blossoming teenaged girl at 15, there were some moments when I felt I was failing as a mom just because my daughter had episodes of sudden mood swings and crying spells, locking her up inside her room.

I talked to several moms who have teenagers at home. They shared the same experiences with me, telling me that teenagers are somehow feeling lost and in search of their self-identity. Upon further research, I learned that, indeed, teenagers go through a stage where they are trying to resolve their life crises that include identity crisis and identity confusion. I also came to know that this crisis represents the challenge to find balance between their uniqueness or individuality and trying to "fit in" or have that sense of belonging to a group, particularly of the same age group.

When I finally tried to convince my daughter, who was aged 15 at that time, to tell me what her problem was, she said that she felt she had no friends, which made me really think that she must have been suffering from identity crisis and feeling some sort of social isolation.

Social standards in our society have played a big role in the youth of today.

I may have not realized that I'd actually suffered from identity and isolation crises in my youth, just because I felt the pressure from my parents' own sets of standards.

Only after I'd exhibited independence, I started to discover my self-identity up to the point of being married and having children of my own. However, in the process, I felt as though I was losing it again, because I was caring for more lives first before looking after myself.

And being a mom and a wife, it's just natural to think about our family's needs first before ours. Is it required? No. It's just simply automatic in every woman because our identity is embedded in having that strong motherly instinct of compassion, love, and selflessness.

## Self-Image

According to Wikipedia, self-image should not be confused with self-awareness, self-concept, self-consciousness, self-perception, self-esteem, or self-confidence, because self-image is the mental picture—

generally of a kind that is quite resistant to change, which depicts not only details that are potentially available to objective investigation by others such as physical appearance but also items that have been learned by that person about themselves, either from personal experiences or by internalizing the judgment of others.

Furthermore, Wikipedia noted four types of self-image as:

1. Resulting from how an individual sees oneself.
2. Resulting from how others see the individual.
3. Resulting from how the individuals perceives others see them.
4. Resulting from how the individual perceives the individual sees oneself.

I've created a distinct self-image for myself based on what I've accomplished, because I've embraced who I really am through mastering myself and knowing what I'm capable of doing. My impression about me, my hopes and dreams, and what I think and feel about myself helped me in creating that vivid self-image that I now use to pursue my dreams and aspirations in a very positive and impactful way.

When I started to invest in mastering myself through a self-mastery program, I was able to project that image of being successful, according to my own definition of success.

Because being successful requires a positive outlook in life—be it through the way I think, speak, or act—people can see that change and regard me as a positive person due to my self-image.

In other words, because of the way I see myself or think about myself, people can see and feel that in me as well. My self-image is my inner mirror that reflects from the inside to the outside.

### Self-Esteem

Experts define self-esteem as the overall sense of self-worth or personal value, embedding that confidence based on his or her own abilities.

I believe that self-esteem is not natural, but it's rather developed over time. We were all born without it, and many factors have contributed to high self-esteem in some people.

I think that my self-esteem started to develop when my late grandmother told me about my potential of becoming a good medical doctor based on her observations. I never knew that her simple comment would really have impacted my life.

I was made to believe that, indeed, I'd be a good medical doctor in the future. I remember asking my parents to buy me toys and dolls to play around like that in a medical setting.

Eventually, I entered university and enrolled in a four-year pre-medicine program to prepare for my lifelong dream. I initially planned to specialize as either a pediatrician or a gynecologist after pre-medicine. In the process, a relative commented that I won't be able to make it to proper medicine because our financial status won't allow it. It later dawned on me that she was right. I gave in to the idea instilled in my head. I then lost interest to pursue and excuses plagued my thoughts.

Therefore, self-esteem can either be developed or depleted.

As a mom, it is important that I help my children build their self-esteem and confidence by nurturing them with unconditional love, fair treatment, kindness, understanding, and encouragement.

Because parenting is said to be based on standards, rather than the emotional component of raising the children, developing their self-esteem becomes the most crucial part that needs to be given utmost attention, especially when parents try to follow the overabundance of advices from experts, fellow parents, and the environment.

I used to implement strict rules in my household for my children, as I was brought up that way. I previously had the impression that, because I wasn't an obedient daughter, I'd be labeled as a disgrace and a failure in the family.

After all my failures and misfortunes as a youngster, it made me think that there's no way I could regain my confidence back, had I not studied who I really am and mastered myself well.

When self-mastery was introduced to me years back, I had the realization that the "golden rule" really applies — in that you treat others the way you want yourself to be treated.

## Self-Awareness

In its simplest definition, self-awareness is the art of knowing oneself.

But which aspect of yourself should you be aware of best for you to consider that you know who you really are?

According to Daniel Goleman, a psychologist, self-awareness is to know more of one's internal states, including his preferences, resources, and intuitions, which means that it emphasizes the inner faculties of one's wellbeing, such as our thoughts and emotions.

According to studies, the majority of the population is not self-aware.

Why is that?

The answer is simple. Most of us unconsciously do the things that we do because our minds wander to another time and dimension rather than what's present here and now. In other words, we are most likely to be on the "automatic pilot" mode in that we tend to be "not there," and are missing out on what's really happening in the now.

Self-awareness is also helpful in determining why you became the person that you are today, including the why you think, feel, and act.

In essence, it is what you develop when you pay attention to your expressions, behaviors, and reactions towards yourself and the people around you.

Being self-aware as a mom and a wife enabled me to better understand my children and my husband. And because I've accepted the fact that people are different— even though my children are my own blood—this helped me to respect their uniqueness and personalities and create a harmonious nest. My interpretations of their behaviors began to change, which marked the beginning of more peaceful and healthier interactions inside my household.

Being self-aware also afforded me the ability to create the life that I wanted for myself through identifying what I'm capable of doing, which are aligned to my passion and purpose. Just because I have exactly identified these things, I am able to make necessary changes and adjustments to arrive at my desired results and achieve my goals for my family and myself, which I describe as SUCCESS.

## Self-Acceptance

The most successful, happiest, and wealthiest people in the world have a sense of self-acceptance.

What is self-acceptance?

It is simply defined as not just being aware of your strengths and weaknesses, but also accepting them both as part of your massive growth. Both should be used to better hone you towards the best version of yourself.

Have you been to a job interview? I assume you have, as most of us have. And it has always been part of the hiring process to state your strengths and weaknesses. But, whenever I go to interviews and would hear this part, I would start to frown inside, because I know for a fact that interviews cannot truly measure a person's worth. Actual performance on the job can.

When I had mastered myself and accepted who I am and what I know about what I can and cannot do, I began to appreciate the importance of having clarity in all things related to my progress as a mom, a wife, a woman, and an entrepreneur.

My very specific example of my weakness is putting too much attention to details in that I sometimes tend to overwork myself at the expense of my own health and other tasks that I need to accomplish first. However, I have dealt with this challenge by starting to delegate work so that my productivity can increase without compromising the quality of the outcome and its efficiency.

Another example of my weakness is not being interested in the technical side of a task. I also did not like numbers, but I would rather have my energy put towards what excites me more, such as content writing, talking to people, coaching, and so on.

I fully acknowledge my flaws, and embracing them never became a hindrance that prevented me from pursuing my passion and discovering my life's purpose.

The Johari window is one of the techniques I really appreciated when I had my own self-mastery program in the past. It helped me to gain an understanding of how I perceived myself and how other people perceive me. It also guided me to better understand my relationships with myself and others around me. This was originally created by psychologists, named Joseph Luft and Harrington Ingham.

The Johari Window tool also aids in assessing the four facets of every person's personality such as: Open, Blind, Hidden, and Unknown personality. This helps us to grasp our distinct personal characteristics so that we can be aware of what part of our personality we reveal to the outside world.

Oftentimes, our strengths and weaknesses require different sources of validation, which can be Divine—validation from within—and validation from the outside.

If you're a believer of God, Divine validation is evident from the teachings in the Bible found in some verses.

One specific example is from the book of Galatians 3:26 that says, "For you are all sons of God through faith in Christ Jesus." When you have accepted that you're a God's child, then you know that everything that happens to you are God's doing and through His grace and mercy for you.

The *Open Personality* window includes the strengths and talents that you know and others know, such as your core competencies and even your limitations.

Self-auditing is needed to validate the traits that you have, which you and others know altogether.

The *Hidden Personality* window includes the traits that we don't know, whereby it is important that we seek feedback from others about our traits, personality, talents, and limitations or weaknesses. But validation can also come from your own self and can require some further explanation from other people. It is how people look at you based on their perspective—feedback from people who you think know you best.

The *Blind Personality* window includes the traits that you know, but you are unwilling to share with others so that they won't know about them. Specific examples are your skills, weaknesses, intents, interests, motives, or inner drives that you want to hide from others due to fear of rejection, criticism, or judgement.

The *Unknown Personality* window depicts those traits that you and others don't know about yourself such as your potentials, new skills and abilities, new talents, new realities, and new opportunities. This part of one's personality can be amplified or enhanced through the help of self-development programs, mentorship, workshops, opportunities, and other self-help programs for growth to unleash one's potentials and core gifts.

There are so many powerful tools that experts use to help a person better understand himself towards accepting what his strengths and weaknesses are that he can use for his massive growth.

### Self-Disclosure

Self-disclosure is basically communicating or letting others know information about you to another person. Information can either be positive or negative and can include feelings, goals and dreams, aspirations, failures, or fears.

Experts say that proper self-disclosure promotes a positive attraction. When two people inform more about themselves, they become easily acquainted and comfortable in each other's company.

Self-mastery really helped me to build my relationships with myself and other people.

Knowing my true self-worth and accepting who I really am enabled me to disclose myself to others easily without any pretentions, hesitations, and prejudice.

Let me remind you, beautiful woman…

Anchoring in that one great truth that YOU are indeed precious, will make you shine the brightest and share that light with others who need it, especially to the people you care about the most.

*When I started to accept that because I am not a perfect mother, and my children are not perfect either, I realized that we can still be effective as a team to make things work for us."*

# CHAPTER 4

## Queen Bee and My Nest

*"Being a MOTHER is not about what you gave up to have a child but what you've gained from having one."*
*— Unknown*

A QUEEN BEE GENERALLY MEANS BEING A LEADER OF A FEMALE group, but this has been useful and applied to several social settings such as business, schools, communities, and so forth.

Let me borrow this title for a second, as I'll be talking more about my function as the leader in my household.

I am the Queen Bee of my nest.

### Changing the World

"I want to change the world."

I heard this line so many times in different speeches and even read it in many articles in the past.

But can we really change the world?

Do we need to be a superhero to do that?

When I was a kid, I wanted to become a superhero with super powers, who fought the bad guys.

Growing up, I realized it was fictitious.

When I was married and had my own children, the meaning of world became more personal to me. My family became my world.

We can't choose our families. They don't choose us either. They are the people we are gifted with.

There's no such thing as a perfect family. In fact, there are disagreements, misunderstandings, and fights. But we'll do everything we can in our might to love and protect them.

I'm pretty sure that you and me—we have the same world, our respective families.

So, if our family is our world, then I can honestly say that we all have the capacity to change our world. But hey, not literally to change who they are. So, let me explain further.

I was inspired by Mother Theresa's famous quote that says, "If you want to change the world, go home and love your family."

As parents, we have the obligation to love, nurture, and protect our children. As a mom, being the light of the household—so to speak—I endeavor to give my full attention to them, provide their every need as much as

I can, feed them with proper nutrition, guide them to become better persons, and to just be present for them.

My second child, Danver, who is sixteen at the time of this writing, was naturally shy when he was a small kid. He was easily intimidated by loud people around him. He would end up isolating himself from his peers. I knew it was his nature, and I also knew that I couldn't just change him the way I wanted to. By being there for him, I'd always let him know that he's not alone. I'd always remind him how much he's loved and appreciated.

However, at one point, I'd noticed his interest in arts and music. I then slowly encouraged him to learn how to play the piano. Subsequently, we enrolled him in a music school. Thank God! Danver had finally been part of the St. Michael's Choir School in Toronto, Canada, a semi-private Roman Catholic School, which is among the six choir schools in the world that has been affiliated with the Pontifical Institute of Sacred Music in Rome. He'd be a part of the school's trips around the world for musical concerts and performances.

I'm happy that I never gave up on him. And believing in our children, even though they couldn't see what they were capable of, is one of the ways in which we can change our world. Feed them with love, positivity, and encouragement.

It just takes someone to believe in your children. And that's You!

Because of that, my quest to change my world has become deeper.

I'd finally decided to leave my corporate job to attend to my family full-time, with my last day at work on August 15, 2016. I was excited but afraid. I have to admit that it was one of the toughest decisions I've made in my lifetime. I was afraid — afraid of the unknown. My love for my family, especially my children, was my DEEPEST WHY; the reason why I do the things I do now.

As I always tell everyone, I'm a wife and a mom first, followed by whatever role I chose to play after that goes second.

### First School, First Teacher

I was raised without privileges and luxuries. We had a modest lifestyle. We would just have enough for the basic needs and didn't have extra money to buy what we wanted.

My father was an ex-OFW (Overseas Filipino Worker) in the Middle East for almost three decades. He would barely come home for a vacation, and because of that I never had the chance to get to know him well until later in my life when he retired and went back home for good. My parents worked their butts off, but I wondered why we were hardly able to get by. And from what I'd witnessed, I lost faith in hard work. I thought it was a scam.

My mother had the most influence on me growing up. She taught me how to survive amidst poverty, how to be financially responsible, and how to endure pains.

She was my first teacher, and our small house was my first school.

My mother didn't finish school because her parents were poor. When she had us—her children—she stopped working and decided to be a housewife. She helped my father earn a living by weaving baskets at home and selling it. My late grandmother taught her to weave baskets, and my mother also taught me. I would help her from when I was eight years old until I relocated to the city for my university degree.

Hard work still didn't impress me, just because we were still broke. But what I've realized from that experience was believing that I can make things happen to change my life. I've accepted that my mother wasn't equipped with the same mindset. And so, I geared up for something better.

I was able to finish my university studies and passed my licensure examinations despite financial struggles. Prior to that victory, most days I could barely secure money even for my public transport to and from school.

To me, it was just the beginning of a new chapter in my life.

It may have been far too different from the way I live my life now, but I teach my children that it's not enough to just work hard. Believing in themselves and taking immediate actions have to go with it. I teach them the value of my continuous quest for growth through self-development and education, and to never settle on what they think is comfortable.

And I'd come to appreciate my hard experiences in the past, such that I have valuable lessons to teach my children (as my students) because I'm their first teacher.

On the other hand, had it not been for the love and sacrifices of my own mother for me, I won't be able to move forward and see what's in store for me.

I know this truth: My children didn't choose me to be their mother, and I didn't choose them to be my children either, but given another chance of a second lifetime, I'd still love to have them again. Those little voices that constantly say, "Mommy," are music to my ears.

I'm not a perfect mom, but there's one thing I know—I trust that I am exactly what my children need. I love them with all of me.

As moms, our love for our families cannot be measured. But how do we really find balance in being both soft and hard?

Do you find it quite difficult to answer this question? I think that this is what we all have to master.

Let me share with you how I do it that works best for my family.

## How to Properly Groom the Household

As a stay-at-home mom, I felt that all expectations are thrown at me by every member of my family, which I don't really take in a negative way. However, sometimes, I'd just feel that I can only do as much, especially when overwhelm comes to play.

I used to have a list of household rules that my children should follow. But this is what I've noticed. The more I set standards, the less they follow.

And I found a better solution to deal with it.

Kindness makes our children feel loved. Shouting at them when they don't follow does more harm than good. It creates wounds to their being, all the more when it occurs on a regular basis.

When I started to accept that because I am not a perfect mother, and my children are not perfect either, I realized that we can still be effective as a team to make things work for us.

Reflecting upon my own childhood helped me realize this one big truth, and here it is:

That there is the most powerful force in the universe. It is called LOVE.

I have a cousin from my mother's side of the family. He's much younger than me, but we grew together in our neighborhood. My uncle didn't treat him right; he verbally and physically abused my cousin. I witnessed it.

While I felt sorry for him, I could only support him morally because I wasn't in the position to help him at that time. Years later, I visited him and asked him how he was. He admitted to me that he hated his father and even attempted suicide, but he was able to move on. And I asked him how he did that.

I was struck by his answer. He said he moved on because his mother loved him.

I ran out of words to say and we hugged each other tightly as we both cried.

The same powerful force works not only in children, but in a spouse or a partner.

As a woman and a wife, my tendency is to be emotional almost all the time. And I know my husband doesn't like it. He doesn't like drama. I'd turn a small thing into a big deal, thus leading to a fight. But things changed when my husband stopped provoking me. Instead, he'd just let it pass and ignore my tantrums. And because of that, I stopped provoking him, too! Of course, we still argue, but not to a big extent. We'd talk it out immediately and then everything returns to normal.

When we operate from a place of love and kindness, there's no doubt that something mystical will happen. It's contagious. It's magical. You may not see the changes in a snap, but the seed, once planted, grows every single day, nurtured with caring gestures of words and actions. And before you know it, good fruits are ready to be harvested.

## Mothering Different Age Groups

Mothering is already a tough job in all aspects—physical, emotional, mental, financial, and so on.

And hear me on this. What about adapting to different age groups?

Not just one, not two, not three, but four! Four children to raise—two teenagers and two toddlers. Aside from their ages, their genders and respective personalities require unique needs.

Being able to adapt to four different personalities is what makes mothering not only challenging but interesting.

I realized that I'm not only a teacher to them, but rather a student as well. I get to learn from every encounter with them each day. New discoveries unfold on a consistent basis. Because motherhood is not provided with a manual to follow, everything just flows naturally and spontaneously. And one outstanding trait of being a mother is that she is able to readily understand her children's feelings, actions, verbiage, and thoughts—even without being told. She just knew it by using her motherly instinct.

When I gave birth to my first child, I was in total amazement as to how I was able to bring her precious life out to this world. I appreciated my new role even more when I discovered much in the process from breast-feeding, to enduring sleepless nights, changing diapers, putting my child to sleep, and all those new-mother lessons. Sometimes, I wondered, while I was looking at my daughter—who happened to be my firstborn—where did I get my strength from? Because I never thought I'd be able to do what I was doing.

And here's what I'd discovered.

Every woman in the world was born with her motherly strength. And it is activated once a situation requires it.

A woman is naturally compassionate—whether she's mothering her biological children or not.

Every time I talk to my daughter, Sophia, I use a specific language fit for her such that she can understand me better. With my second child, who is a boy, I use another language for the same purpose—to understand me better. I use another language with the third child, and then another with the fourth. Because I embrace their uniqueness and different personalities, I am able to identify their specific needs, and complement them accordingly.

I've accepted the fact that, even though my children all came from me, they still have their respective individualities—preferences, likes, and dislikes.

Understanding and embracing their distinctiveness enables me to perform my motherly duties at best.

Sometimes, in those moments of overwhelm and not knowing what to do, you'll find your motherly strength ready to be activated.

## Self-Mothering

And so, I'm a wife to my husband. A mother to my children. A woman to the society. I change my hats each time to fulfill such roles.

But have I not forgotten anybody to mother, too?

Yes, I forgot ME!

Therefore, I need to mother myself as well. That's right!

And what does it really mean to self-mother?

Okay. Let me elaborate more on this.

In reality, the word "mother" is not just a noun but a verb, which primarily means to nurture. It is, therefore, an action. In fact, to mother or to nurture is not gender-restricted, which means that it's not only for a woman. A man can also mother or nurture. Because of that, anybody can be a mother to anyone.

And yes, we can even mother our own selves.

For the purpose of further illustrating my point here, I'd use self-nurturing more, instead of self-mothering.

When I had been exposed to poverty and the hardships I experienced in my life at a very early age, I had the strong desire to change the course of my destiny. I had that inclination to make things happen for me and my mom. When I tried to look back, I realized that I was, in fact, already self-nurturing through my positive affirmations directed to myself for inspiration.

I stood to the fact that hard work wasn't enough, and believing in myself as well as taking action would do the job.

You may have not experienced lack of any sort—finances, relationships, loss—but I know that unconsciously, you've been self-nurturing all the time. You're just not aware.

Sometimes, we get to learn to mother ourselves because our own mothers are not available. And maybe, just maybe, they didn't have the drive to nurture themselves either. Not because they didn't like it, but maybe it's not really there.

To summarize, mothering is not just for a woman to a child (or children). Mothering knows no gender. It knows no race, color, or social status. It's open to anyone who is ready to give it and to receive it. You are included. You can mother yourself, indeed!

And one of the best ways to demonstrate self-mothering will be discussed in the next chapter — SELF-LOVE.

*Self-love is the beginning and the master of all forces in the universe, because the more you love yourself the more you are capable of loving others. The more you like yourself, the more you'll like others."*

## CHAPTER 5

# Secret Two Revealed: Self-Love

*"You owe yourself the love that you give so freely to other people."*
– Unknown

SELF-LOVE OR LOVING ONESELF IS OFTENTIMES REGARDED AS displaying selfishness, conceit, and vanity.

I used to believe that, too!

Being a mother requires a substantial amount of positive thoughts, words, feelings, and actions. But hey, don't get me wrong. Don't feel bad for having negative feelings at some point. What makes it bad is when you let these negativities destroy you, paralyze you, and prevent you from shedding your light upon others.

Negative vibes create fear. And the best antidote for

fear is love. You don't want to transfer fear to the people you care about the most, including yourself.

Therefore, you need to have love in yourself to combat that negative feeling.

Be the person you want to attract.

Remember, you can only give what you have. So, self-love is mandatory.

Self-love, or Philautia, is a type of love that is within oneself. However, oftentimes, it can also be associated with narcissism (from a mythology that a man, named Narcissus, fell in love with his own image).

But why self-love?

Self-love is the beginning and the master of all forces in the universe, because the more you love yourself the more you are capable of loving others. The more you like yourself, the more you'll like others.

What we see in others is a reflection of us.

For instance, you have this colleague at work whose attitude pisses you off. He always complains and never appreciates anything. I know, it's reasonable that you get pissed off as well. It's a negative energy. It's contagious. And you may feel that sometimes his negativity is directed at you. But when you know exactly who you are, you're able to empathize readily, because you are equipped with love, kindness, and understanding. You just don't take things personally.

Another example.

Imagine you're in a grocery store. You suddenly stop by the fruit stand to buy some red apples. On the surface, they all look fresh, shiny, and crispy. You pick that one apple on top. It looks really good. Then, you pick another one, but you notice that it's rotten on one side. Will you take it?

I bet you won't! You dug down the pile to find better ones.

Of course, you won't eat blemished, rotten, second-grade apples, right?

My point here is you don't want to ingest anything bad that can cause you harm, be it either inside or outside your body. Obviously, rotten foods can make you sick.

Aside from unhealthy foods, there are also things you can't physically see or touch that can still harm you.

Unforgiveness, anger, envy, doubt, self-limiting beliefs, resentment, and a million more negative thoughts that you can think of.

I know it's easier said than done, but operating based on self-love will bring you more clarity, direction, and awareness about what's not only the right thing to do, but also the kind thing.

**The Oxygen Mask Theory**

You may have boarded an aircraft in your lifetime. Before take-off, the cabin crews will teach the passengers to put the oxygen masks on in case of an emergency landing.

And here's the interesting part.

You may have heard about encouraging the adult in-charge or the responsible party when boarding a plane with a minor or a dependent to put his/her own oxygen mask on first before helping others.

Why?

The Oxygen Mask Theory is a demonstration of a real-life situation that teaches us the importance of equipping oneself first so that he/she can help others, which is a win-win situation in the end. This is where others fail to understand and rather regard it as an act of selfishness.

And it just makes sense that if you do this, you'll be in a better position to assist others who need it. Loving oneself also works the same way. If you don't have that level of love for yourself, you are in no position to give it away or share it either.

### The Right Kind of Mindset

If there's this right kind of mindset, do you mean there's a wrong mindset as well?

Let me define what mindset means first.

In its simplest terms, mindset is a set of attitudes or a way of thinking that creates a specific outlook in every situation.

The definition of mindset can be different depending

on who you ask; I believe our definition depends on the goals or end results one wants to achieve.

I cannot simply judge what a right and a wrong kind of mindset should be because everyone is different.

What do I mean by this?

Every mom is almost always after her children's best interest. Parenting comes into play when I'd like to teach my children a certain value to practice.

For financial literacy, I model the right mindset as to how money works. Some parents may think it is way too early to teach that, but my household is open to discussing almost any topic in a manner that they will understand at their level of understanding and age.

We, parents, as the first teachers to our children, transfer the wisdom that we learned from self-help tools, mentorship, and our past experiences, because we feel the need to encourage them to develop not just the right kind of mindset, but something better than that—the growth mindset.

I have a toxic relative in that no matter how hard I try to please her and make peace with her, she always ends up attacking me. But I can't seem to avoid her, as she's related to me by blood. I developed an interest in studying and learning more about how the human mind behaves. I came across a book, *Mindset: The New Psychology of Success,* by Dr. Carol Dweck, which talks about two basic mindsets, namely a growth mindset and a fixed mindset.

According to Dr. Dweck, a fixed mindset assumes that our character, intelligence, and creative abilities are static and that we can't change them in any meaningful way. On the other hand, she indicated that an individual with growth mindset believes that intelligence can be developed, resulting in even higher levels of achievement.

I started adopting the growth mindset; not just to understand others, but towards my self-mastery. I wanted to unleash my full potential and core gifts.

Fixed mindset, on the other hand, is the kind of mindset that defines people who believe that they are the way they are and will die that way. They find it hard to change or go to the next level due to their fear of criticism, rejection, or threat.

But here's the interesting part.

I have some areas in my life to which I apply a fixed mindset—driving a car, for instance. I never drove a car because I'm fixated to my belief that I'm nervous, I can't take it, I'll not be able to learn it, and I'm not interested in it.

You, too, may have been practicing a fixed mindset in some areas of your life. And you'll know it when you say something like, "I'm not good at that" or "I'm too old to join the group," and so on.

Is a fixed mindset wrong, then?

It's a yes and a no. If you go back to the definition of mindset, it is a set of attitudes or a way of thinking that creates a specific outlook in every situation.

I don't like to drive a car or even learn it. Is it wrong? Of course, not! Because I know I can still go to places by taking the public transport. And it doesn't make me less of a person or prevent me from accomplishing something if I just commute.

A fixed mindset only becomes wrong when it's obvious that you refuse to change a belief system or practice that can ruin your progress and sabotage your own success and the success of others.

## The Value of Self-Care

When I was still single and free, without children, my time and money were all mine. I felt the universe was mine. I'd go to shop until I drop; I'd go to movies, shows, and events regularly.

I believed that I was good at practicing self-care back then.

Until I got married and had kids, I realized that self-care is not just about what makes me happy, but rather what should also keep my body, mind, and spirit healthy.

It should not only include the physical aspect but also practices to promote a healthier lifestyle, including regular exercise, balanced diet and good nutrition, proper sleep hygiene, relaxation, rest, meditation, massage, and so on.

One of the complaints I hear from fellow moms is lack of time to even think about themselves, and I can totally relate to that. Having four children plus a husband in my household requires my full energy and attention from sun up to sun down.

Is there really a way to sneak out and go to the salon or spa, at least?

Because of a million tasks on my plate, it seemed next to impossible to think about indulging and relaxing, especially when overwhelm strikes. However, I realized that if machines become tired, then humans can, too! When I learned to change my practices and manage my time properly by way of mastering my priority matrix, self-care has been part of my daily activities.

In turn, it prevented me from experiencing a sense of burnout where that feeling of being unable to take anymore or nearly giving up is no longer an issue. Giving myself time also helps me to re-focus and then do things better than before.

Another thing that I believe is very important to note is that self-care reduces the effects of feeling stressed out, which enables you to functioning at full capacity.

I also give myself a mini-splurge such as going to the mall for a short walk or even window-shopping while eating ice cream. This frees me up from my daily routines for some time so that I can be recharged, and then go back to my daily grind feeling energized.

## Healthy Network

Jim Rohn, a well-known motivational speaker, puts it this way, "You're the average of the five people you spend the most time with."

In other words, we become the kind of people we hang out with the most: their behaviors and attitudes, the way they think, and even their results.

And now you say, "Anna, you're a stay-at-home mom. So, you hang out with your children and husband most of the time."

Good point!

It's true, of course. Remember, I told you that we can't choose our family in the same way that they can't choose us, right?

Whether we like it or not, we hang out with them — our partner/significant other or spouse and our children.

But can you also remember about a relative of mine who puts me down? I chose to stay away from her. Love her from a distance. When a relationship becomes toxic, then it requires a second thought.

This is equally important with the kinds of people we associate with in terms of business, self-development, faith, and other areas of life; those we choose to hang out with, talk to, and socialize with.

Every human's social need has to be fulfilled to grow, inspire, and love. And our children will see that from us.

It's just good enough to say then that, "Show me your friends, and I'll tell you who you are."

Imagine you hang out with moms at your kids' school who complain all the time. "Oh, life is too hard." "Everything is expensive." "I don't think we can get out of poverty." "The weather is too bad."

If you're hearing these complaints over and over again, what could happen to your thoughts? Your words? Your actions? Rest assured, you'll end up complaining as well. Worse, you'll bring those complaints home!

As the Holy Bible says, "Faith comes from hearing." – Romans 10:17

This only means that we tend to believe in what we hear. That's why we have to be mindful of the people we network with.

We have the option to choose who we want to associate with. But how?

First, law of attraction applies in everything you think, feel, and do—which simply means that you get to attract into your life whatever you focus on—including people, money, events, and so on.

Second, when you have self-mastered and known who you really are and what you want to become, then you'll exactly know what kind of people you need to be surrounded with. For example, if you want to learn more about entrepreneurship, of course, you'll find a network of like-minded people who are engaging themselves in entrepreneurship. It makes no sense to be surrounded by people who are into arts. That's a complete waste of time, energy, and effort.

I've had some experiences in associating with the wrong network; I was able to learn how to set boundaries. I have to warn you, though, that there may be instances in which some people you initially consider the right network for you end up taking advantage of you. Be wary. Be extra careful.

Learn to say no when it doesn't feel right. Did I previously mention about gut feeling or intuition, the sixth sense? Use it.

Of course, practice due diligence at the same time.

## Spiritual Connection

I don't know about you, but I'm a firm believer in only one God. I trust in having that Divine connection with my Creator, which I can consider a form of my spirituality with another being other than myself or others. Yes, I can't touch and see God, but I know He exists. It's called faith. And my faith in the Supreme Being is how I live my spiritual journey for the most part.

On the other hand, spiritual connection can also be with your romantic partner, where you both have that deeper sense of knowing and understanding each other —your goals, dreams, and aspirations. Getting to know each other on that level strengthens your bond to create that spiritual kind of love towards one another.

My husband and I are spiritually connected to one another—strong enough that I feel extremely comfortable when he is around, and he admitted that he feels the same way, too.

Another indication that my spiritual connection with my husband is there when my emotions are linked at the heart level with his, and not just sexual.

More than the physical need, intimacy also plays a big role in improving our spiritual connection such as spending our "us time" together, even if it just means sitting on the couch, watching a movie together, and so on.

I also know that we're spiritually connected when a certain stimulus results in a simultaneous reaction, which gives us that sense of an indescribable bond.

Another form of spiritual connection is having that nature-connectedness. I used to not be a firm believer in spending time outside with nature, but when I tried to do that for the first time, I had that feeling of peace and calmness inside me. Experts say that exposure to nature is good for a person's health, wellbeing, and happiness. Connecting with nature also promotes self-reflection about appreciation, gratitude, and solitude.

# CHAPTER 6

# Tearing Down the Hardest Wall

*"A bird sitting on a tree is never afraid of the branch breaking because her trust is not on the branch but on its wings." –*
Anonymous

It seems very common that everyone experiences those moments of unrelenting frustrations, only to find out that these frustrations stem, not from somewhere outside, but rather from our very own SELF, which is the hardest wall to tear down.

How is that?

Well, when I embraced self-mastery, I learned not only to know myself well, but also to pick my battles.

What do I mean by that?

I hold the remote control of my life. I can choose when and how to react or respond to a given situation. And frustrations usually come from unmet expectations.

Did your husband or partner forget your anniversary? Or did you receive your child's report card with a failing mark?

Do you think being mad will help you feel better?

Pause for a second and reflect.

Why become hard on ourselves and our loved ones when there's a better way?

So, what's the better way, then?

I'm not a relationship expert. But here's what I know straight from a woman's heart.

Peace of mind is the highest human good. The better way to deal with overwhelm, noise, and confusion, is to pause. It's that simple. Just pause. If you need to go out and breathe some fresh air, do so. You want to write it down? Go ahead. Find your place of peace. You need that space right there and then.

It's easier said than done, I know. But practice makes perfect. Or fake it until you make it. But I promise you, you'll never regret it.

We also feel like hitting ourselves hard and then pose millions of questions inside our brain about what has gone wrong.

Negative emotions, frustrations, and self-doubts are believed to be by-products of our inner enemy. Being able to acknowledge that there's this monster inside of us can help us find a way to tear down the hardest wall, which I will talk about next.

## Self-Limiting Beliefs

There are certain beliefs that we have acquired from people and events before us, our families, culture, traditions, core values, practices, lifestyle, religion, and so on.

Some liberate us to improve and help us grow, while others limit us to be the best versions of ourselves.

But let me elaborate further on the latter—the self-limiting beliefs.

Limiting beliefs are those that constrain us in so many ways, by affecting the way we think, speak, and act.

These beliefs develop when we perceive ourselves as something sans evidence or proof, or when we hear others' negative comment about us. For example, starting from our own homes, when our parents say, "Being an engineer doesn't suit you." Or something like, "You can do better than that when you change your program."

More likely than not, self-limiting beliefs are negative. It's the voice in your head that states you won't get good results or you won't succeed. In fact, these self-limiting beliefs encourage us to have a fixed mindset that there's no room for improvement.

In addition to keeping you from growing, it paints yourself as a victim. A specific example is when you tell yourself that because you're born poor, you're not going to succeed and that you'll die poor.

But the good news is that you can do something about the self-limiting beliefs.

Acknowledging that they exist is the first step. Being aware equips you to prompt a sudden shift in your mindset that will lead to a stronger and better outlook in life, and creating a brighter future.

Taking action to change that belief is the next step.

Third, maintaining the kind of mindset you need to achieve your goals and dreams is the last step.

It's okay to fail. Get up. Try once again until you've broken that wall. And break free!

### Self-Doubts and Fears

Are you plagued by self-doubts?

Where do you think they came from?

You start with a sense of hesitation to believe that you're capable of doing something when you think that you're not good enough.

You may recall that we talked about fear in *Chapter 5, Secret Two Revealed: Self-Love.*

Fear is, in fact, the absence of love. However, when there's self-love, you feel that sense of abundance and you are at peace with yourself—thus, creating more peace outside that naturally radiates to everyone with whom you share a close encounter.

Self-doubt is one of the manifestations of fear. When

you're plagued with self-doubt, you feel powerless, unworthy, empty, and useless.

Doubting oneself develops not only from feeling that sense of lack from within, but it is also influenced and amplified by others.

And I'm guilty of it. The sad truth is, even if we didn't intend to do so, we, parents, contribute to our children's self-doubts. Although I may describe it as being overprotective at times, it poses more harm than good in their motivation to do more.

One morning, my eight-year-old son asked me if he could join the track and field in his class. Instead of my instant approval for his request, I told him that he may be too small for that sport and won't be able to finish even the hundred-meter dash. With my son's persistence to join, I finally agreed. The tryout finally came, and he fortunately was able to make it. He officially joined and, in fact, won second place.

It gave me a very painful realization that being a mom, I should be the first person to believe in his ability. I should have given him my permission right away without having to make him feel inadequate for it. Although my real intention was to protect him from being hurt, I was, in fact, hurting him more because of the self-doubt I projected onto him, which I knew impacted him deeper than I could ever imagine.

Self-doubt is our personal parasite. The "I can't"

attitude is just another way of saying, "Yes, I'm a loser," or "I'm incompetent." More harmful than that is the fact that you are self-sabotaging your innate capabilities even before trying. It emerges from a feeling of fear—fear of failure.

All forms of fear are negative emotions that create feelings of danger, threat, or pain.

When I had decided to leave my corporate job to be an official stay-at-home mom, I was afraid—afraid of the unknown. Since I was gainfully employed as a corporate worker, doing 9-to-5 job, finances were one of my biggest concerns due to a huge cut in our household income.

However, fear can sometimes be a good thing, too! They say that courage is not the absence of fear, but rather what you do in spite of its presence.

I used the courage I have inside of me.

Others say, "Do it afraid." Because only in trying will we know if it works or not. We have to be reminded that by not doing what we're afraid of is way riskier than actually doing it. Fears of failure and rejection are the most two common fears we have.

You'll never know unless you try.

### Self-Worth

Is there a set of standards to measure one's self-worth?

I asked the same question before as to how we should really give value to a person.

Do we use certain metrics to justify one's value?

In today's social standards, we often notice that a person's self-worth is measured by how much money he has in the bank, his income, his material possessions, position in the society, politics, affiliations, and so on.

A couple's common source of conflict is the comparison of income they both bring to the household.

According to the married couples I'd spoken to, when the wife brings home more revenue than the husband, a sense of insecurity on the husband's part arises most of the time. Sometimes, it's the other way around. Just because women are given the inherent role of running the household, they are not expected to be in the limelight or going up the corporate ladder, which makes them earn lesser income than their husbands.

It saddens me when moms come to me and complain about how they are being dominated by their husbands just because they contribute less income to the household. Although I cannot say with certainty if this is cultural, or just a lifestyle or a preference, it only validates that income is really used as a means to measure a person's worth.

Husbands or male partners have to know the gravity of running a household and the fact that it cannot be matched with any amount of salary or monetary compensation.

I loved my job, seriously. I was an intrapreneur—an expert in my field. It was where I felt comfortable as I performed every detail of my job. However, I chose to leave it for something I knew better; something that I knew would fulfill my purpose—and that's being always physically present to my family more. Because of that, I knew with certainty that I had to change gears. From commute to telecommute. From corporate to home-based.

Did I think myself as less of a person?

No!

Instead, I felt empowered with higher self-worth. I was able to find myself. I knew exactly what I wanted. And I made things happen.

The other usual occurrence these days is counting a person's self-worth based on one's background, culture, race, education, and achievements.

I was once a victim of racial discrimination at work. I was doing medical transcription, which required excellent fluency in English—both written and spoken. One of my former co-workers questioned my being fit to do the job, because English is not my first language.

Did I retaliate?

No, I didn't. Just because I knew my self-worth. I knew exactly what I got!

I'm a motivational speaker and a published author. And this book that you're reading right now is a proof. So, I'd rested my case.

Gender orientation is also being used to value a person's abilities.

My late grandmother once related a story to me that, during her youth, women were not allowed to work in offices or be involved in businesses just because women were only confined to their respective houses to take care of their families while men were the ones who were out and engaged in social affairs such as business, politics, and leadership.

Other physical aspects that people use to measure value include build, body size and shape, and appearance. Skin color due to race is also used to measure self-worth. Some people judge others with regard to how well they can do a certain task just because of the impression that color matters.

### Sense of Lack

In the book, *Maximum Achievement*, Brian Tracy, talks about a very important mental law, called The Law of Correspondence. This law tells us that our outer world is nothing more than a reflection of our inner world — "as within, so without."

It is a principle that says our current reality is a mirror of what is going on inside us. In other words, nothing in our outer lives can change without first making changes on the inside, which is applicable to both positive and negative feelings and thoughts that obviously manifest themselves either by the words we speak or the actions we take.

One specific example is the continual sense of lack, feeling unworthy, or having no sense of purpose in life.

When we complain about everything in the world, our outer world will be a place of chaos and complaints.

In essence, a sense of lack or unworthiness is a feeling that almost everyone experiences at some point in his/her life, myself included. And what is even worse is when we continue to think more about it, we even reinforce and magnify that sense of negative thought that invites more negative vibrations and creates a ripple effect in our life.

When I was still employed, my manager asked me to create a presentation about the possibility of transitioning from an analogue transcription to digital. Although I may have the expertise of doing the actual job, I must admit that I didn't have enough knowledge about the IT side of the operation. I was on the verge of declining the request until I realized that nobody in my department was more fit to do it, because I was the one in-charge and had been doing the job for over twenty years.

I was initially scared because I felt I was lacking the technical side of the presentation. Fortunately, despite that sense of lack, I did it afraid. I bumped into a friend on the subway days before the presentation, who happened to be an IT guy and knew something about my subject matter. We'd discussed it over a cup of coffee, and he gave me some helpful information. In short, the presentation went well and I was commended by my bosses.

Because I still proceeded to do it despite a feeling that I lacked something, I was able to attract the exact person I needed for the said presentation, who helped me to accomplish the goal.

There are so many specific examples in my daily life that are obviously happening through the power of the Law of Correspondence. We have to alter our attitudes and beliefs inside of us in order for our outer world to change.

We often would have the urge to ask people to change for us, which is next to impossible. Changing ourselves first on the inside by altering our responses to stimuli will push others to change.

And then you ask, "How can others change when we change ourselves first?"

My father and I have something in common. We are more likely to argue, especially in the middle of a heated conversation. We would end up being in the losing ends. My guess was that my lack of a fatherly image for the longest time—because he was away for almost three decades while I was growing up—must be my way to draw his attention. Lately, after mastering myself, I knew that I didn't have to make my point straight away to win the argument, but would rather let it pass and preserve my relationship with him.

Our sense of lack may manifest as our way to fill in a gap in a relationship, unfinished business, untapped potential and opportunity, or anything that makes one feel empty and incomplete.

## Anxiety Attacks and Depression

Anxiety attacks and depression know no gender, age, status in life, or religion. They can strike anyone. Their manifestations differ from one person to another. And even worse, the victim sometimes doesn't know he/she is affected by it.

Anxiety is a common emotion. Not everyone is spared from feeling anxious every single day. When life is already a challenge, feeling nervous is a common manifestation. When we worry too much about anything—which causes panic attacks—we feel overwhelmed and that can greatly affect the way we think, speak, and behave. Although this may be regarded as short-lived sometimes, entertaining such attacks can certainly derail our focus, productivity, and results.

If not addressed properly, this can lead to a more serious condition, called depression.

Depression is a mood disorder that affects the way one thinks, feels, speaks, and behaves. It causes severe sadness, hopelessness, and lack of interest in things he/

she previously enjoyed doing. A depressed person also experiences difficulty with sleep, concentration, and focus.

When I'd suffered from post-partum depression (PPD) after giving birth to my fourth child, I thought that my feelings of irritability, anger, and other negativities were just the result of exhaustion and sleepless nights related to breast-feeding.

We can help somebody who's undergoing any type of depression only when its root cause is identified and the disease itself is addressed. However, it's sad to know that depression is not given utmost or serious attention for the most part.

Also, a solid support system from family members, friends, community, and experts can greatly help.

Depression may also differ in terms of the severity and frequency.

Either way, depression and anxiety attacks ruin a person's future. And addressing it properly can save a person's life.

## Hubris

Everything that is done in the extreme is not good. The same is true with how we display ourselves.

Previously, I have talked about how self-limiting beliefs, doubts, fears, a feeling of unworthiness, sense of lack, and depression as well as anxiety attacks can be detrimental to becoming the best version of ourselves. On the other hand, being on the other side of the spectrum of being overconfident with extreme manifestations of ego or arrogance can also harm and lead to one's downfall, which is a term referred to as "hubris."

The word hubris came from the Greek word hybris, which means "wanton violence, insolence, outrage" or "presumption toward the gods." In Greek mythology and drama, hubris was an affront to the gods, as no mortal should believe himself to be more powerful than the gods, nor defy them. Therefore, Greek gods often punished characters who displayed hubris.

Hubris, according to Wikipedia, describes a personality with a quality of extreme or foolish pride or dangerous overconfidence, often in combination or synonymous with arrogance.

According to the Holy Bible in the book of Proverbs, "Pride leads to destruction, and arrogance to downfall."

I think everyone has a touch of hubris in his/her persona. We see hubris exhibited very commonly in our daily encounters.

You may have had a colleague at your workplace who looked down upon you, feeling that he's much better than you are. You'll suddenly feel a sense of incompetence because of that.

A person with hubris personality trait enjoys a powerful position, and overestimates his capabilities.

Another strong manifestation of an individual suffering from hubris is not wanting to acknowledge help or accept others' opinions, and thinks that everything is in his/her favor.

Many famous and wealthy celebrities and politicians in our society today have displayed hubris, which led to their significant downfall. They thought that because of their popularity and power, they'll remain impenetrable.

Having too much pride leads to tragic flaws. Not being able to swallow one's pride or exhibiting humility can definitely be one of the hardest walls to destroy.

Examining oneself is the key to determining what needs to remain and what needs to be torn down to re-build a better YOU!

*Although I believe that God is still the greatest provider of my needs, my life is a masterpiece as a result of a 50/50 partnership between myself and Him."*

# CHAPTER 7

❦

# Secret Three Revealed: Self-Made

*"Care about what other people think and you will always be their prisoner."*

– Lao Tzu

GOD CREATED THE UNIVERSE AND EVERYTHING IN IT. WE, humans, are the highest species He made. According to the scriptures, we were created in His own image and likeness.

Humanity (a woman) is given the power to co-create a precious life of another human being. Her body is designed to carry it in her womb for nine months and then bring out to the world through childbirth.

I feel so blessed to have exercised that power four times in my lifetime. I stand as their steward, which means that I'm responsible to nurture, raise, and love them.

What a serious and big scope of responsibilities!

To put it in another perspective, God gave me four because He knows I can handle four. He gives us tasks that He knows we can handle perfectly.

Although I believe that God is still the greatest provider of my needs, my life is a masterpiece as a result of a 50/50 partnership between myself and Him.

I used the gift of free will to grow into the person I am today—a self-made wife, mother, and woman.

What is meant by being self-made?

In its simplest form, it is a process of becoming successful or rich by one's own efforts.

There are two elements to reach success. Success is an inside job, which means that the intention and action should come primarily from oneself first.

Second, success cannot be done alone. It is the result of a collective effort of people with the same goals, who can be your healthy network of like-minded people and your mentors or coaches.

You may have heard about successful people who are said to be self-made millionaires or even billionaires. And the common starting point among them is they had nothing to begin with: no money, no connections, and no knowledge. They made it from the ground to the top, using the two elements of success I mentioned above.

On the surface, one can reasonably say that a person is self-made by looking at his net worth or the number of accolades and recognitions attached to his/her name. And these are not bad.

However, being self-made is not limited by those good things we see or hear. A person can be considered self-made through his/her self-reliance. Of course, it doesn't mean that he/she doesn't ask for others' help. What I mean by that is, a self-made person, who is also known as self-reliant, knows how to use his own resources first, rather than those of others. A self-made individual knows how to handle himself very well and is independent.

## Finding Happiness from Within

Happiness is a vague word. It may mean so many things in our vocabulary. Sometimes, it may be described as tangible proofs of achievements such as a dream house, a new car, and so forth. Others define happiness as landing the job of his/her dreams.

But if we only define happiness from this point of view, would it mean that underprivileged and homeless people are not happy?

I have, in fact, seen disabled and handicapped people who, from the looks on their faces, seem happy and positive.

When my youngest son was only about a few days' old, he could readily recognize my voice and face. When I would talk to him, he would cast his most precious smile to me.

Based on that, I could tell that happiness is a natural thing that comes from within.

Again, as my story goes back to leaving my corporate job of over twenty years, being able to stay at home, and earning a living through my home-based businesses, I found genuine happiness in my heart.

Why is that?

Because I've identified and served my deepest why — my family.

Pursing a career or promotion is not bad at all. If that's what defines your happiness, go for it.

Every person is different. And preferences may vary, but happiness shouldn't be forgotten.

I'd experienced buying material things I thought would satisfy my needs and longing, only to find out that what really made me happy was already in front of me.

Basking in simple pleasures such as eating ice cream, telling jokes, and going to the mall creates a remarkable aura that can be transferred to the people around us.

Happiness is a decision. And you already have it. Because it's just within you.

And as the saying goes, "The best things in life are free."

## Stillness and Inner Peace

The world that we live in right now is so noisy and full of movements in that it makes us unable to listen to the important messages that we are supposed to receive, and to appreciate the beauty of stillness and solitude.

Solitude (or silence) enhances that sense of balance and clarity to our thoughts, thus leading us in the direction of our own destiny.

I will reiterate that I'm a mom to four. And you must have created a picture of how my household looks like with four children of different age groups. Starting from our used utensils and plates in the kitchen, to our dirty laundry each morning, washroom mess, and so on every single day when my family members are all gone to school and work, I can only say that I just want to just sit down and stare at the aftermath, wishing that they could clean and organize themselves without touching a thing.

I may have exaggerated it, but I'm happy with my roles as a mom and a wife.

Stillness is only required when things seem to go erratically or uncontrolled.

Yes, my house may be physically messy, but the voices of my children and husband are music to my ears.

After fulfilling my significant roles at home, I spend a moment of silence and give myself that sense of inner peace. I saw its importance in order to create harmony with myself and others. Operating with that sense of calmness—albeit the external world seems so unorganized—creates a happy household and a happy mom and wife, indeed!

Inner peace is not the absence of noise; it's the ability to be in the state of calmness and serenity despite outer chaos. It's my experience to know myself best.

## Emotional Intelligence

Emotional intelligence (EI) or emotional quotient (EQ) is a very important skill that refers to the ability of a person to manage and control his/her emotions and those of others, discern between different feelings and label them appropriately, use emotional information to guide thinking and behavior, and manage and/or adjust emotions to adapt to environments or achieve goals.

Experts say that EQ is more important than one's intelligence (IQ) to arrive at true happiness and success in life, be it career or family. Being able to have that high level of ability to understand other people is one of the manifestations of having mature emotional intelligence skills, which include social skills, empathy, and adaptability.

Although motherhood doesn't really require any qualification—to do the toughest job in the world—developing emotional intelligence will definitely create a happy household.

I'd mentioned several times that I raise four children of different age groups, two teenagers and two toddlers — one girl and three boys. Their exposures to different people outside our house make it more difficult for me to adjust to their mood swings, tantrums, likes and dislikes — the list can go and on. Had I not learned that I needed emotional intelligence to be adaptable to their uniqueness, I would have gone crazy in no time.

Even playing the role of a wife can for sure be affected after feeling so physically exhausted and tired. And my emotional intelligence can save me from giving up.

Being an emotionally intelligent person can be hard, especially when we're required to practice empathy towards another person and experience their frame of reference or place ourselves in their position. It may be easier to do that for people we love and care about than for those who are not related to us.

## Lightness

It's not bad to set high standards for ourselves, especially when that pushes us to do more, and to be able to achieve our goals and dreams. Setting an attainable expectation is not bad either.

There are times when we set a certain goal and is unmet, we become too critical of ourselves. We can always try one more time or until we hit our desired target.

Being too hard on ourselves can only do more harm than good. Forgiving ourselves also will make a difference to be more positive in life.

I once read in an article that the reason why angels can fly is because they are light.

I'm guilty of being hard on myself sometimes. I tend to beat myself up too much at my own sanity's expense.

We are all humans, and nobody is spared from committing mistakes. When I commit mistakes, my tendency is to dwell on them for a long time. There will be moments when I can't get over an unfavorable event, which feels like eternity to me. I regard myself already as a mess when things don't go the way I wanted it to turn out.

I usually become frustrated when a deadline is not fulfilled or my expected results are not achieved. And my course of action would be to sleep late at night just to hit a specific deadline, hoping for better results. Although I know that it's part of the success process, I should have realized that a day or two of extension to meet the said deadline is acceptable, especially when it's not a life-and-death situation.

So, how and when can we experience lightness in our lives?

As a person (woman), letting go of toxic people in your life, regardless if they are related to you or not, can bring you lightness and a sense of ease.

Experts also say that you'll know a relationship is healthy when there is laughter.

Not dwelling on your bitter past is also good for you.

Motherhood will be lighter by accepting your family wholeheartedly, no matter what they do and who they are.

As a wife, embracing everything about your spouse or partner—including his flaws—will create lightness in your relationship and marriage until death do you part.

I'd asked a married couple how they managed being together for more than thirty years. The husband said that love is not enough, but laughter will make it even stronger. Sense of humor makes their relationship interesting and fresh each day.

## Spirituality

Spirituality is actually a broad concept with different perspectives. However, I believe that it is a sense of connecting to something much bigger than ourselves, which in turn creates that hunger to look for a deeper meaning in life.

When we think about spirituality, religion comes to mind first. Although it can be as close to a Divine connection or a relationship with God, I've learned that it can also be a strong connection with nature, a meaningful event, other people, or even to oneself.

When we connect with something bigger than ourselves, we'll experience positive emotions, thus creating a deeper sense of wellbeing, reflecting acceptance, compassion, gratitude, and contentment.

I must admit that times still come to me when I feel uneasy, confused, restricted, or incomplete.

And I engage in activities such that I can go back to being a self-made individual.

Prayer, meditation, reflection, and connecting with nature help me much. By doing so, I am made truly aware that there is this Infinite Intelligence present as the source of all creative expressions of life for ourselves and others.

## Giving and Forgiving Freely

To give and to forgive are two different things.

The former is the act of granting another person something we have. It can be both in the form of material possessions or merely sharing feelings, advice, and comfort.

A self-made individual has the ability to give freely because it's his/her nature.

In one of the priest's sermons on a Sunday afternoon, he said that there are three kinds of givers: A grudge giver who gives, but the heart opposes the act. A duty giver is someone who gives out of obligation. A thankful giver is one who gives out of a thankful heart. Giving can be in different forms—tangible and intangible. Nevertheless, it touches both the hearts of the giver and the receiver.

Love and kindness should be the main intention why we give, and then we further articulate the intention by our selfless act of giving through the tangible forms such as money, gifts, mementos, etc.

We have all experienced being hurt and also hurting people, be it intentional or not.

I initially didn't understand when they said that forgiveness is something that you don't do for others, but rather for yourself. And then I realized that failure to forgive is self-cannibalism, because it eats you up alive due to anger, resentment, and the like.

Forgiving is the best thing you can do for yourself. And now I agree that it's absolutely right.

According to a recent study in the *Scandinavian Journal of Psychology*, happy people are more forgiving than unhappy people. Forgiveness is a decision that we translate into action, which makes us feel better, and converts the negative feelings and thoughts into positive ones.

A self-made individual doesn't hold grudges and bitterness, and is willing to let go instead of thinking about revenge or hurting the offender back. It takes courage to say, "I forgive you," especially when the gravity is hard enough to damage one's life, either physically, mentally, and emotionally.

As Mahatma Gandhi puts it, "The weak can never forgive. Forgiveness is the attribute of the strong."

## CHAPTER 8

# Role Models vs. Runway Models

*"Children have never been very good at listening to their elders, but they have never failed to imitate them."*
– James Baldwin

BEING A MOM (OR A DAD) CARRIES TONS OF RESPONSIBILITIES. And making our children follow us can only be easier when we set a great example to them. It's not always easy to be a perfect role model for them, as there are different factors that make our decision-making not aligned to what we want to teach them. Sometimes, it may not be in our favor to what our children want, but, as parents, we would like to make the right decisions for their best interest, all the time.

Without consciously knowing it, from the words we utter to the actions we take, our children are watching us. And then we wonder why they have attitudes that make us quite angry, only to realize that they are, in fact, from our own doings—"monkey see, money do," as they say.

## Getting Real

We can't be happy when we live in lies; lies that cover us from the reality of life. We can go past the bad ones and forgive ourselves and others who have contributed to such fate, but it is worth moving forward and being real instead.

Becoming real is not just about accepting what it is, but rather realizing and understanding what's happening based on true facts of the situation, instead of hoping for what is impossible to happen or likely to happen.

Sometimes, when life demands that we are real, we tend to be out of control and forget about the respect for ourselves and others through the harsh words that come out from our lips for the sake of being real.

For a married couple, it becomes tragic when both of them deny the fact about what's going on as to why problems come out, without addressing the root cause of the problem.

I should admit that when I see my parents fight and sometimes wouldn't talk for a while, I'd just stay away from their world and not intrude, because I know it's just between them. However, I believe that it's also my right to ask—as part of our family's relationship—to know what's really going on.

Many of us pride ourselves on being authentic, but authenticity can be a tricky term. We sometimes express ourselves as being honest in our opinions, feelings, and thoughts, only to realize that we are, in fact, not communicating authentically. Judging or blaming others, and in some severe cases committing character assassination, falls under the presumption of being real.

Being real involves a sincere effort to go deeper inside ourselves to uncover what we're feeling, thinking, or whatever it is that we're experiencing and then communicating that.

Pausing for a moment and checking in with ourselves is required before reacting to a certain stimulus or responding to either an attack or a praise, whatever the case may be.

Covering up—sometimes for our kids and spouse— may not always help in maintaining healthy relationships. In our every day life, especially when tough decision-making is required for the best interest of our children, it makes it even harder to come up with something between being real and what's best for them.

My husband and I decided to enrol our son, who is 16 years of age at the time of this writing, to a semi-private, boys-only school in Toronto as I mentioned in the previous chapter. I must admit that the expenses, including tuition fee, musical instruments, uniform, transportation, trips, and other miscellaneous activities at school that are required for his musical grooming, hurt our budget, especially now that our eldest daughter is in university. We may have wanted him to continue attending the prestigious music school, but we have to be real and tell him that it's causing us some financial challenges. It hurt me personally as a mom, but I made my son understand that it's in everybody's best interest, because there are four of them, our children, who need financial support from us.

In the end, after adapting to his new school, he even thanked us for exposing him to a new environment, without losing his interest in arts and music.

Being real requires two key points such that all parties will benefit. Mindfulness is the first one, as it allows us to attend to our experiences as they are, without judging ourselves or anyone else. Immersing ourselves into our now enables us to experience our connection with our own self from moment to moment. When we do that, we allow the other person to see our authenticity, which encourages them to be as real as much as they should.

Kindness is the second one. We may have known people in our lifetime who are kind but not quite emotionally honest. I may have been initially hurt as a mom, anticipating that my son won't be able to accept his new sets of friends, his environment, and his new school, only to find out that he's happier where he is right now. I believe that my son and I'd both benefited from being real in the first place, just because we'd also taken into consideration his other siblings who need financial support from us as well. He was receptive to my message, with my genuine sincerity and clear intentions from the heart for the greater good.

Being able to communicate with people, not only through words but in action in a kind way, makes a difference in the process.

The beauty about every human being is his/her uniqueness. And being real makes a person stand out from the rest, just because nobody can ever be the same.

### Natural Beauty

When I was in the elementary school, I would always stay in the library for a long time because I loved to read my favorite comic books. One of my favorite characters was Wonder Woman. Her super powers, strength and her physical body, beauty, shape, and build amazed me. I once wished to be just like her!

She was just so perfect, and I felt so inferior. It gave me the impression that superheroes were meticulously selected by their gods because they were so darn perfect.

Years past, and I also began to be interested in reading fashion magazines. The same feelings had me wondering why these women were so pretty and I wasn't.

I don't know about other cultures, but where I grew up, I was led to believe in the idea that beauty is based on color, height, nose structure, eye size, waistline, bust size, and other physical attributes.

Generally, there is a set of standards as to how beauty is measured.

Going to the department store also exposed me to how beauty is defined. I'd see huge images of beautiful models of different beauty products from head to toe. Having that fantasy of somehow acquiring even a tiny bit of their goddess looks, I'd end up buying cosmetics in the hopes that I, too, can look flawless and attractive.

Although I believe that enhancing our natural and God-given beauty is not bad through wearing some colors here and there, the feeling of envy, because other women look better, is another story.

Should beauty icons in fashion magazines, pageants, modeling arenas, and TV commercials be called role models?

A role model is a person who serves as an example of the behaviors, attitudes, and values that can be imitated by others, especially when these traits are associated with a certain role. Generally speaking, when I think about what a role model is, he/she is a person whose character traits and deeds stand out—not purely physically—that can serve as an inspiration to other people.

I came across an inspirational talk online about how the beauty business and industry has become ugly these days. I was intrigued by the speaker's opening remark about it, and so I continued to watch it for a better understanding about what she really meant. In her speech, she said that most women think they are not beautiful, merely because the images presented to them are not real, but rather manufactured, which serves the beauty industry well. They'd throw promises to their clients, that using the product would make them look many years younger, slimmer in no time, and every other transformation you can think of from the natural body to something magical, just as seen in magazines.

I'm not against beauty products. I use them, too! In fact, I'm thrilled to use them for parties and special occasions.

We are gifted with free will. Provided that we don't violate any of our rights or other people's rights, do what makes you happy—what is just, what is right, what is kind, and what you most deserve.

But here's my point, woman! Nothing beats your natural beauty. You are already beautiful inside and out. You don't need to worry.

## What Social Media Had Done

I could still remember some thirty plus years ago when my father was working in the Middle East as an OFW, and I was about eleven or twelve years old; my mother would patiently wait for my father's letter in the mail after about a month. She would then write back and mail it, only to be received by him after the same amount of time. An overseas phone call was very, very expensive back then. Communication lines were always disrupted, and it would take several transfers from one operator to another before a real one-on-one conversation between my parents could happen.

Their communication was hard, all the more their long-distance relationship. Happenings were not up-to-date.

Thank God for our innovative discoveries where modern communication services began to broaden their reach and improved their efficiency in a shorter period of time. The invention of analogue cell phones to digital, and then to touchscreen smart phones, had only proven that everything now is very, very possible. What is more interesting is that two or more parties can communicate in real time and face-to-face, regardless of the time zone and location. It's, indeed, very impressive!

In the 1990s, through a series of continuous virtual experiments conducted by several experts to fully endorse the World Wide Web (www), it had been a huge success not only in every office space, but in every home. It then led to the birth of the modern internet. Internet amplified the use of electronic mails (e-mails), causing the traditional snail mail almost obsolete.

Social media, primarily Facebook, has been part of the world's popular culture.

The use of social media platforms has both pros and cons. The founders aimed to promote fast and real-time interactions with family and friends across the globe. Because we know that communication is one of the biggest needs to strengthen human relationships, it served its purpose through these creative solutions.

The experience of being engaged in and part of such a community became the easiest and most sophisticated. And the best part, it's free! However, I have noticed— and I'm guilty of it—that social media has become our open diary where we post almost everything publicly. Although I cannot judge the intention of each person who posts photos or anything related to emotions, lifestyle, and preferences, it sometimes bothers me to see even some sensitive issues posted in public that goes beyond what's supposed to be private.

I still believe in the timeline posts that most of them are intended to inspire; however, what social media had done to us is quite alarming. When digital applications (apps) have not yet been introduced or widely used, photos, for example, were just produced as they are. Free photo editors that are built in our smart phones and other electronic devices to enhance our images such as skin color and body parts, turns out to be an instant cosmetic alteration done digitally in a few clicks. It masks the attributes of a person's natural appearance.

Why in the first place do photo editing or photoshop?

Again, I cannot really judge people who are doing it. I can only speak for myself. I really wanted to look good. Yes, I'm doing it. And I don't think it's bad. However, when I examined myself deeper, I asked myself why. I'd be honest to admit that I'm afraid of what people will say about me. I'm worried about being judged based on my imperfections. This, I think, is what makes it bad—when my reason for using the photo editors to make me look good is to encourage others to like me or praise me not because of who I really am, but because of the digital cosmetic enhancements.

Just because everyone is doing it and it's the trend doesn't mean we really have to do it. I must also admit that I felt good when I have edited my photos and posted them on Facebook and people would hit like and write awesome comments. However, on the other hand, I knew it was not 100 percent me. I hid my imperfections. I made myself look better and covered who I really am. I looked so flawless, with a slimmer face, contoured nose, and blemish-free skin.

But did it really make me happy in the end? I couldn't say absolutely yes. My photo editing served its purpose and I achieved what I wanted, but I knew it wasn't purely me.

In an effort to just show only my beautiful and admirable side and what's happening around me, I am guilty of not being 100 percent real, thanks to the alterations on the surface to project that picture-perfect scene in the imagination of those looking at it.

Am I really being a role model to my group? Or am I just feeling like a runway model on Facebook?

As a person, I realized that it doesn't matter at all what other people would think of me. Because, at the end of the day, what I need to always work on is to become my children's role model, without having to alter the natural beauty I'd been given.

## The Perfect-Mom Fantasy

If we only accept the truth that nobody can ever be perfect, I believe it would be much easier to be real.

The same applies to our role as a mom and, of course, a wife.

Being able to carry a precious life inside a woman's body for roughly nine months is already something special that no man can ever do. Since motherhood doesn't come with a manual to read before getting started, it's understandable that a new mom would experience overwhelm, confusion, and all that. But I have to tell you that, even if I am a mother four times in my lifetime, I still can't say that I'm a "pro." I may have plenty of experiences, but everything that I know now just happens as it comes. I still believe that I have much more to discover in the process that no manual can ever teach.

Based on my observation, other moms feel frustrated when things don't go their way or when they compare themselves to fellow moms. One specific example is when it seems like a competition, involving their children's test results or performances at school. And this is when they'd start to feel as though they needed help to become a perfect mom!

I must also admit that, being a stay-at-home mom, it is worse than I thought. Just because everyone in my household expects me to provide everything for them, my whole plan for the day is usually ruined. It is even more frustrating when you don't know who should be attended to first, just because you know everybody is important.

Let me take you on a tour of my life for a second.

Imagine a mom with four children and a husband. From waking up as early as 5AM to prepare their breakfasts and lunches for school and work, to the whole aftermath in my kitchen, followed by home-based businesses to attend to afterwards, I'd still have other errands to do in between such as cleaning the house, paying the bills, doing the laundry, and dealing with other unexpected chores. What about time for myself?

I searched for ways to address this issue. Upon further study and implementing it in my own life, I was able to find a solution for this. I identified the challenges as a person, a mom, a wife, and an entrepreneur; I found a solution, and then implemented it, which I still do up to this point.

I mastered the implementation of proper time management. And I've listed the seven tips that I personally do for effective and proper time management that you can copy, as follows:

1. **Priority Matrix.**

   I'm a huge fan of writing down notes, more so when it contributes to the results I want to achieve in any area. Many actually call it the "to-do" list.

   I encourage you to make sure you plan things out at night before you go to bed. It makes a huge difference when you have a roadmap for the next day.

   Decide what you are first.

   What do I mean by that?

   As I mentioned, I'm a wife and a mom of four, and these are the roles I decide to play first. And it's non-negotiable. My top priority and use of my time every single day are associated with these roles, so that I can accomplish everything that needs to be done.

My other roles as an entrepreneur, a careerwoman, and others are next in line.

When the kids are already at school and my husband goes to work, then that's the only chance I'd work on my feet, doing other stuff for my businesses, and self-development activities.

2. **The 5AM Club.**

Switching from being a night owl to an early riser, though hard, gave me great benefits—better overall health, productivity, and a sense of clarity, to name a few. I now rise before or at 5AM every day. You may choose your own specific rising time, as the whole idea here is to be up and awake earlier than your old rising time OR while half of the world is still asleep such that more things are done. The 5AM club concept was introduced by Robin Sharma, a leadership and performance coach, who teaches productivity.

It's easier said than done, I know, but I recommend that you observe proper sleeping hygiene, as lack of sleep sabotages productivity, leading to bad time management.

Our physical body needs to be energized and recharged to prepare for our daily grind.

Waking up early enables us to exhibit a healthy lifestyle, because we'll have more time to prepare healthier meals, more time for proper hydration, and, of course, more time for exercise – thus, developing a more effective and a productive YOU.

3. **Do NOT multi-task.**

There's a debate between multi-tasking and to *not* do multi-tasking.

Experts say that multi-tasking often does more harm than good. And our brain can only handle one thing at a time, unless you're a rare hybrid.

However, multi-tasking in a 9-to-5 job, for example, answering the phone while checking e-mails, can be done all at the same time effectively, especially if that is required in the job. And it's actually another topic to discuss.

But when it comes to multi-tasking outside of employment or around the house, it just makes sense to do more tasks altogether, such as reading a book or cleaning the house while spinning your washing machine or thawing a piece of meat for cooking.

**4. The Art of Letting Go.**

Not everything you consider to be important is really important. Literally speaking, decluttering is an art, and it's indeed one of the ways of letting go.

If there's a "to-do" list, there should also be a "not-to-do" list.

So, what to let go?

I'd say PLENTY!

You let go of time wasters, such as too much entertainment from TV, video games, and social media.

You let go of toxic people that drain your energy.

You let go of physical clutters in your house to create more breathing space. This creates more clarity about many things and saves time for more important matters. Less clutter, more time for productivity.

Anything that hinders your growth—let it go!

**5. Create your "ME" time.**

As primary caregivers of our household, especially moms, we oftentimes neglect the importance of having an exclusive "ME" time. It literally means spacing out from the noise around us for some time.

My "ME" time is when I usually experience my "aha moments" for myself, my family, or my business.

Reading self-help books, short trips to the mall, and wandering in nature boost my creativity big time!

Organizational and productivity tools.

At this present age, digital apps are widely used for productivity and organizing tasks as well as schedules.

I admit it: I'm an old-school type. I'm more inclined to using notebooks, sticky notes, store (or free downloadable) calendars. Using these types of tools help me tremendously to manage my time and money as well.

You may choose to find tools that suit your needs, lifestyle, and preferences, so long as the results favor you best.

7. **Buy Time.**

Yes, you read it right. Buy time! This is another way to say delegate and distribute.

As I have previously mentioned, I know exactly what my roles are that I play first: a wife and a mom. Just because we all have very, very limited time, I've come up to the idea of buying other people's time so that I can focus on what matters to me more—my family.

And here's what I really meant.

I continuously hire Virtual Assistants (VAs) to do most of the administrative tasks or those that I'm not expert at or interested in doing, which can be on a project or contractual basis, for my business.

While being the "Queen Bee" of my nest, I'd have other people work for me instead, to leverage my precious time while I attend to my household.

Then, you say, "What if I don't have money to pay people?"

Don't fret. I used to think that way, too.

Have you ever forgotten the ever-famous line that says, "Time is gold?"

If time is gold, then it means money. You waste time, you waste money. As simple as that.

In other words, I'd rather pay someone else for things that don't really contribute to my productivity and making money.

Yes. Create more money, so you can also buy time!

And if money is an issue for now — which it is for many — I encourage that you follow the tips I've shared here. I know that you'll arrive at the same position where I am now, enjoying more time freedom.

Yes, buying time is my top secret! I really do buy other people's time to delegate and distribute the work as much as I can.

Once you've done it, you can really appreciate how beautiful time freedom is, thus leading to a happier life with little-to-no stress, especially when dealing with a million things on your plate.

Again, let me summarize the SEVEN (7) tips for your effective time management, as follows:

1. Priority Matrix.
2. The 5AM Club.
3. Do NOT multi-task.
4. The Art of Letting Go.
5. Create your "ME" time.
6. Organizational and Productivity Tools.
7. Buy Time.

I believe in the pure intention of every mom I know about providing all the best they can, but I just realized that in doing so, we tend to run in both directions in an effort to try to carry out everything, leaving us with frustration and overwhelm.

I decided to let go of the perfect-mom fantasy. It doesn't exist. Teaching our children to contribute in the house, on an age-appropriate level, and being responsible, is our way to groom them to become more independent and useful persons when it's time for them to live on their own or settle down.

I also appreciate being in the network of fellow moms, but sometimes I experience this feeling of overwhelm from the overabundance of advices and opinions, which made me think that I am not good enough as a mom. When comparison comes in from the way other moms run their households, to disciplining their children, budgeting, and buying what-seemed-to-be-better brands, that feeling of inadequacy on my part as a mom sets in and creates that sense of guilt, as though I'm not doing the right thing for my family.

This persisted until I realized that every household is unique, preferences and lifestyles are different, and the needs may not be the same for each family, albeit we're in the same neighbourhood. This is what I know: I can never be perfect, no matter how hard I try. But one thing is for sure, I always do my every effort to nurture and care for my family and love them to the best of my ability. I can never perform as a mom to my kids by copying other moms, as I want to be their role models when they, too, become parents in the future.

## What Is Real Success to Me

When I was about five years old, different strong beliefs were embedded in my brain. I was fed with the idea of success as someone possessing fame and money, plus the highest educational degree one could ever have. Two of the professions, that were always in my top three choices, were a lawyer and a doctor. For some reason, I never had the inclination of becoming the former, as I was more interested in the latter.

Because I wanted to become successful, I was reassured, especially by my family, that being a doctor would fulfill my goal. I took a pre-medicine program and finished my bachelor's degree in Medical Laboratory Technology. Fast forward, due to different challenges, specifically financial, I did not end up entering medical school. I felt, as though, I was a failure.

Until I married my husband and had a family of my own, I realized that a professional degree cannot solely be associated with a person's success.

When I became a mom, my perception of success shifted to my family. When I see them happy and fulfilled with the love and care I provide them, then I know I'm already successful.

My own definition of success has now changed. Success is as simple as meeting my goals.

And my goal is to stay at home for my family and earn a living at the same time, without leaving the house.

My success now is very much congruent with my goal. And I already made things happen for me and my family.

Being always at home now means you may find me in my pajamas almost all the time, with a few strokes of the comb to my hair every day and a very simple skin regimen. Despite being very basic and plain, I find that genuine happiness and joy as a domesticated type of a woman. But I know I'm successful at what I do now. I may no longer resemble the corporate woman that I used to be, but I'm happy to be my own boss.

My biological mother, for the most part of her life, focused on us, her family. I believe that she must have influenced me in my decision to leave my job and imitate her somewhat, because I find that genuine happiness in her when she takes care of us.

I cannot say with certainty that my only daughter—when it's her time to raise her own family—will do the same that my mother and I did, but I believe that by showing examples, I may have instilled in her the value of being the role model for the next generations to come; that family is not just an important thing, but it is everything.

# CHAPTER 9

# *Changing the World*

*"You change the world by being yourself."*
– Yoko Ono

I USED TO BE SOLD BY THESE VERY COMMON NOTIONS SEEN IN movies that to be able to change the world, one must have super powers; or that you must have one genius idea to treat a rare illness, or create an amazing invention that can make a man disappear in a snap to catch the bad guys. And all these fallacies made me think that there's no chance for me to participate in changing the world and making it a better place to live in.

Until I realized that I don't actually need super powers to make it happen.

Changing the world goes with a huge responsibility. And the question is, how do we do that?

"We can only give what we have."

I don't know about you, but here's what I know. You have a responsibility, regardless. You may be single or married, with or without kids. But you still have yourself to take care of. You are the sole person responsible for yourself. Thus, you can contribute to changing the world when you become the person you are supposed to be. And what do I mean by that?

You may have a sister, a brother, neighbors, community, and co-workers that you can help in any way possible. Helping a person in need is already a way of making a difference and changing the world. Showing kindness is a very, very effective way to do this. It can be just your words of encouragement to a friend who lost hope, an elderly woman who can't cross the street on her own, or a gentleman by the sidetrack who had flat tires. These are all powerful deeds of kindness that can change a person's world for the better.

Indeed, changing the world is simply making a difference in the life of one or two people.

## The Universal Language Spoken

Every living creature communicates, although I don't know the method for each. But there's one way I'm certain about that we humans use, and it is the most powerful language regardless of age, color, background, educational level, or social status.

It's the language of LOVE.

According to experts, only humans have morality; it is not present in animals. This is evident when we negotiate conflicts through socially created values and codes of conduct. Thus, if one reduces everything to its simplest form, then one's behavior may indeed be compared to that of an animal. One distinct characteristic of a human being is his ability to think cognitively and express his emotions such as love creatively, thus being aligned to making considerable moral choices.

What comes to mind when we talk about language is just spoken words. But in humanity, it doesn't provide its meaning to the fullest. Apart from the words we speak, we express our emotions through touch, embrace, objects, or simply an action like calling on the phone, sending a text message, or writing an e-mail.

All humans have the capacity to love, and we can express it even in silence. Why is that so?

We are all created by God out of love, because He is love. And He made us from His own image and likeness, and therefore we are all love as well. And by that alone, we can rationalize that yes, humans are naturally made and born out of love.

Spoken words matter to express our feelings of love, but I believe that action to show it is more important.

I have mentioned about how one can truly change the world.

Words can change a person's world by either your encouragement or despair.

Remember that the tongue has no bones, but it is strong enough to break a person's heart. So, be careful with your words.

## Where Love Should Begin

I won't ever tire of saying that we can only give what we have. If there's hatred in your heart, guess what you can give? Of course, hatred. And if you have love, of course, you will give love.

Therefore, there should be love in oneself first before it can be shared with another. However, loving oneself was regarded by others as being selfish, vain, or conceited. But when you examine it deeper, it is actually one strong demonstration of what someone with love in himself can do to change the world.

Before becoming a mom, I used to think that taking care of myself or at least loving "me" first was being self-centered, only to realize that I cannot give anything to my children when my love tank is empty. In order for me to shower them with kindness, nurturance, and love they need from me, I should have those attributes first. I cannot pour from an empty cup and neither can you.

Being a person, I learned that loving myself is a must to change my world.

And who is my world?

Here's how I define it.

From being single to being married, and from being childless to having four children, my world suddenly changed.

Being a mom and a wife gave me the clear direction as to whom I should give my love to. It's easier for me to express the love I have.

My life is not perfect and not even close to being that way, because I know it can never ever be perfect. The strong force that binds our family together is love, despite our huge differences and imperfections.

But really, how does it begin?

I will answer that question through the next topic, which is Awareness of the Needs.

## Awareness of The Needs

I have previously mentioned about the different needs, not just of a woman but of every man as well. As human beings, God designed us to need affection from others, which can make a person truly happy beyond measure—that no price tag can ever match.

To love and be loved is indeed a great need.

Absence or lack of awareness of our need for love can really plummet a person into deep sadness, frustration, and a sense of unworthiness or meaning to his/her existence.

Being fully aware of the needs of every human being that I have mentioned in Chapter 1 makes it easier for each one of us to make a difference and change the world.

I tend to judge people despite my best efforts not to. It might be just as simple as why the person I came across in the grocery store bought the brand I didn't like. Or it can simply be just a person who cut us off the road, concluding that the driver was rude. Being aware of a person's situation can literally make a difference in the way we act next or respond to a given situation that's right in front of us. This awareness for others sets the stage for a more conscious communication.

I know it's easier said than done, but I also know that it will be a better world if we try not to judge people easily because we can't be certain about his/her own life's struggles, which may be harder than the struggles we currently have.

They say that "We should be kind because everyone you meet is fighting a battle you know nothing about."

Another precious guide to be able to change a person's world is by practicing the golden rule that says, "Do unto others as you would have them done unto to you." Imagine if we could all operate our daily lives inside and outside our homes based on these simple values. I'm 100 percent sure that we can definitely change the world little by little. If we are sensitive enough to the needs of other people, it will surely be a better place to live in—not just for us but for the next generations to come.

## Taking the Lead

I've always believed that success is a vague word in that it can mean something different to every person. And simply knowing that each one of us has what it takes to succeed is powerful enough to translate it into action.

As I mentioned previously, my success is equal to the goals I achieved. And as a mom and a wife, my number one goal was to quit my corporate job, stay with my family 24/7, and run my businesses from home.

With my every effort to achieve that goal in four years' time, I can honestly say that I've already succeeded according to my own definition of success. Everything that I do and have now outside of that achievement is already a bonus. Being a published author, an international speaker, a life coach, and a serial entrepreneur are all just but extras for me, because being a wife and a mom are the two major roles that I consider my top priorities at this time.

And because of the time freedom I gained from the decision I made to make things happen for me and my loved ones, I can enjoy everything I've wished for.

Was it easy?

In all honesty, it was not! Because if it was, everyone could have been doing it and been successful by now. But the difference is that I took the lead; I led myself to the direction I wanted myself to be.

And by fulfilling the roles aside from being a wife and a mom, I am leading others—especially moms and dads who don't know what to do and who seem to be at a loss about how and where to start.

It may sound funny, but yes, you—a woman like you, regardless of your status—can have it all, if only you internalize and follow what I've written in this book.

I love what I do now, as I want to be the voice for others who don't have it. I want the message to be heard, and writing this book is one of the most powerful tools to make it happen. One of my wildest dreams is to reach every woman in the world and lead her by the hand to experience the kind of life she deserves.

You may say, "I'm not a writer or a public speaker just like you, Anna!" Oh yes, I hear you. But hey, you don't have to copy all the things I did. What I'm trying to tell you is that, you are already a leader.

And how do I know that?

Well, you may be a sister, an aunt, or simply a woman who has somebody who follows you, respects you, and treats you as a teacher of an expertise you already know. There's a leader in you. Use that natural gift that you have to change the world and make it a better place for people who depend on you.  Make their lives easier so that they, too, can be a blessing to other people.

Are you into baking?  Teach another mom!

Has somebody asked you to coach that person about a skill you know?  To solve a specific problem?  If yes, then, you're a leader.

Are you good at putting your baby to sleep?  Can you share it with a new mom?  You may think it's very simple, but it can make her life easier.

And there's another powerful way to change the world aside from being a leader, which brings me down to the next topic – Empowerment.

### Empowerment

What is empowerment?

According to Wikipedia, the term empowerment refers to measures designed to increase the degree of autonomy and self-determination in people and in communities in order to enable them to represent their interests in a responsible and self-determined way, acting on their own authority.  It is the process of becoming stronger and more confident, especially in controlling one's life and claiming one's right.

In its simplest terms, I'll use specific examples on what empowerment means to me, as they relate to what I do now.

Being a role model to my children is one way of empowering others. Coaching my students through my self-development program is another way to empower. Speaking to other people either in a small group or to big audiences to motivate them is also an effective method of empowerment. What about this book? I believe you've been empowered by what I've written here so far. Thank you!

By merely inspiring others to do something for themselves such as self-development, taking necessary steps to reach the next level that can be applied either for their business or career, or even a boost in their relationships, can make a huge impact to their inner circle and the community they live in.

So, how can empowerment be used in our daily lives?

Empowerment should actually start from within ourselves.

Daily affirmations really boost confidence and self-esteem. Verbalizing positivity can actually change your life massively, as it feeds your thoughts that then translate to words, to actions, to habits, and then to character, which becomes your destiny.

Only empowered individuals can empower others. And hurt people hurt people.

Again, this goes back to the line, "We can only give what we have."

Your positivity is contagious as is negativity.

Test yourself to be surrounded by whiners, complainers, negative thinkers, and the like for just an hour. What do you think you'd become after that period of time? I'd be sure that, no matter how positive your outlook is prior to that, you'll be infected with pessimism of some sort.

Sometimes, the sad reality is that the people whom we thought would lift us up are actually the ones who put us down.

I initially didn't understand why some of the people I expected to be the first ones to support and celebrate my achievements are, in fact, the ones putting me down. I know this is a common occurrence to many and quite painful to think about, but empowering myself through affirmations and saying no to negative talks do the job for me. Remember, practice makes perfect—so, fake it until you make it.

An empowered person is also the product of the three secrets I've revealed so far, as to how you, either woman or a man, can be absolutely happy and have it all:

Secret 1: Self-Mastery
Secret 2: Self-Love
Secret 3: Self-Made

Having it all sounds dramatic, but really it just boils down to being your best version. As the saying goes, "Be yourself; everyone else is already taken."

And here's what makes it more exciting. When you are the best you, you can definitely follow my next point easily.

So, read more...

## Pursuing Your Passion and Life's Purpose

What do you call that one thing you're willing to do, even if you don't get paid?

Well, it's called passion.

Every human being is passionate about doing or pursuing something.

What about your very reason why you exist?

It's your life's purpose.

Now the question is, "How do you discover both your passion and your life's purpose?"

Passion and purpose are interconnected in many ways. It's important to never lose sight of your passion for anything that will amplify your purpose.

Since age ten, I had this entrepreneurial spirit in me, although some say that this oftentimes runs in the blood or may have been inherited from one generation to another. However, there were no entrepreneurs in my blood line — not even one.

I remember when my late grandmother asked me at that early age to help her sell vegetables that my grandfather harvested from the farm in our neighborhood in exchange of a commission from the total sales. I said that, even without the compensation, I'd be so glad to help out just because I want to interact with people. I would find joy in my heart from doing so, especially for my beloved late grandmother.

I started to dream about becoming a medical doctor when I was five years old, and then I also became interested in being a journalist and a businesswoman. Because my life was prepared to becoming the former, I took a program related to becoming a medical doctor.

While waiting for the results of my licensure examination for the said program and preparing for medical school that same year, which was in 1996, I came across a job posting in our local newspaper that said, "Wanted: Medical Transcriptionist." Thinking that it would be a good source of income to support myself, I applied, was hired, and the rest was history.

Fast forward, I immigrated to Canada with my whole family under the Skilled Worker category using my experience in medical transcription. Shortly after landing, I was employed as a medical transcriptionist in a government hospital in the downtown Toronto area until I established my own home-based medical transcription business, which then led me to leaving my corporate job, and becoming an officially Stay-At-Home Mom (SAHM) in 2016. I then built several businesses from home, which made me the serial mommy entrepreneur that I am now.

Being the expert in my field, I was very much passionate about being the intrapreneur in the world that I was in. Leaving my corporate job was not an easy decision to make, just because I loved everything about my work in the hospital.

After giving birth prematurely at eight months to my fourth child, I suffered from post-partum depression because of a near-death experience during childbirth in late 2012. Because of that traumatic experience, I started to think about what really matters to me as a person, a woman, a wife, and, most of all, a mom. Subsequently, I'd given myself a four-year timeline to transition from commute to telecommute. Thank God, I was able to do it with massive preparation in all aspects and some tradeoffs and sacrifices in the process.

I've discovered my life's purpose that is aligned with my passion, and my heart is so grateful to share my journey with you, and explain to you, my dear readers, how you, too, can do it.

My passion is entrepreneurship and communicating with people. I used my core gifts and experiences to amplify my life's purpose to share what I know with others such that I can help them go from point A to point B. And through the gift of love, I'm able to make a difference in my own world, in the world of my family, and in every person that I meet through my businesses—both online and offline.

What about you?

Have you thought about what your real passion is?

What about your life's purpose?

*"Each one of us is a product of all experiences in life, good and bad, becoming the persons that we are today."*

# CHAPTER 10

# *And the Winner Takes It All*

*"You were born to win, but to be a winner, you must plan to win, prepare to win, and expect to win."*

– Zig Ziglar

WHAT DOES "WINNING" REALLY MEAN?

If I will answer that question, I'd say exactly what I said about success. Winning to me is a vague word, as it is dependent on our own interpretations.

I believe that winning is also a state of mind. In other words, being a winner doesn't mean you never lost or failed at anything. It doesn't make sense, right?

What makes more sense is that, winning is a result of a process that you intend to achieve in the end in your quest for victory. In any endeavor, be it in sports, entertainment, politics, or business, everyone fought against many encumbrances to be able to achieve the position that they've been aiming for. One can never be called a winner unless there's an adversary to defeat.

## Journey to Wholeness

I've come to realize that being poor when I was young was an advantage for me, because I was actually being prepared for greater things. Those were all, in fact, part of my life's training.

I thought that lack of material splurges growing up was a disadvantage or a misfortune. I started helping my mother earn a living at the age of eight. Fridays and Saturdays were my least favorite days, because it was painful to watch my friends play while I had to help my mother weave baskets to sell so that we'd have food on our table for the whole week.

Did I mention that I'm the youngest and the only girl in the family?

It made me think that, "Yeah, what were my older brothers doing at that time?"

I felt jealous inside, telling myself that my other brother must have been favored.

However, I just thought to myself that maybe my mother saw something in me that made her give me more responsibilities despite my gender and age.

It's true that "a journey of a thousand miles must begin with a single step," but getting started with that one step is oftentimes the hardest part of all.

Each one of us is a product of all experiences in life, good and bad, becoming the persons that we are today.

Picking up the pieces again and not knowing where to start is really hard. And it takes courage to do that. But we have to admit that we can't do it on our own, as we all need a solid support system from our spouse, family, and friends.

But what does it mean to be whole? And what or who can really make us whole?

When I was first employed at the age of eighteen after completing university in 1996, I felt, as though, I was on top of the world. I was single and free, with no responsibilities whatsoever. I could literally do whatever I wanted. I felt in total control of my own life. Being officially on my own gave me that confidence and freedom. However, after a few years of being employed and saving enough money, I felt that something was amiss. I just didn't feel complete.

One day, I visited my mother, as she was living with some of our relatives in our small hometown. My oldest brother had a family of his own while my other brother was living independently in the city. My father was still working in the Middle East at that time. I couldn't forget her happiness when she saw me. And it made me think that a person's real happiness cannot just be found in material things but in another person's presence. And I said to myself, "I want kids that I can call my own."

For several years, I imagined myself being a mother and a wife, which truly became a reality after some time.

I found my wholeness in motherhood, and that motherhood supercharged my feminine powers to do more. And if you're a mom just like me, you know exactly what I mean when I say that being a mom is really the toughest responsibility there is, but it's the most rewarding one.

You may not be a mom yet, or maybe you're in the planning stage of becoming one, but I can be sure of one thing; that every person's journey to wholeness is a decision to make. It can be an endless search for some, just because they don't know where to find it.

But let me tell you this.

You have to start somewhere, and you already have it. Look in the mirror, and you'll see it's there right in front of you. The three secrets I revealed to having it all will help you know exactly where to start.

We have all different perspectives, preferences, lifestyles, backgrounds, beliefs, practices, and the list can go on and on. I know. I get it. Go back to the very core of who you really are while asking this question, "What is it that can really, really make me happy?"

Get past the pains, the hurts, the brokenness. Let those old scars and wounds turn into wisdom, and then speak your truth—that you are capable, empowered, and blessed; that you are more than enough!

We are whole when we are ourselves. And let that beautiful self be guided by following your heart and intuition. It's already in you—hidden—that you just need to cultivate and let out in the open.

Raising a family intertwined with different responsibilities attached to it is not easy. That's the truth. But don't be afraid.

Remember, you are a woman! You are wonderfully made. You have what it takes to make things happen.

I should admit that I'd feel empty at times. I initially thought that having kids and a husband to focus my attention to would be just enough to make me really happy and whole, not realizing that I've forgotten one important person, and that is "ME." I failed to include in the equation the words, "I AM..."

I've had that need for self-actualization to realize and fulfill my full potentials.

When I decided to go back to the very core of who I am and make myself whole again, I was able to give myself more as a reflection of my truth as a mom, a wife, a businesswoman, an author, a coach, and all the roles I play today.

When I had equipped myself with empowering tools that I needed to support my very important roles, I felt ready to take everything that life has in store for me.

## Work-Life Balance

What is work-life balance?

According to Wikipedia, "Work-life balance is the term used to describe the balance that an individual needs between time allocated for work and other aspects of life. Areas of life other than work can be, but not limited to, personal interests, family and social or leisure activities."

You know that I had this strong inclination to leave my corporate job and rather be a stay-at-home mom. Because of this, it's now clear what work-life balance means to me. In other words, it's simply doing things that one loves, in good proportion. There's always time for work, family, self, and other activities.

And so, I have to say that the meaning of work-life balance can vary from person to person.

In my own experience, just because I'd started off as a one-man show, operating my home businesses was really difficult. As there was no Bundy clock for time in and time out, I would always tend to work longer than one would normally spend in the 9-to-5 working day as an employee. I had no reliever in the event that I wanted to take a vacation, or even to have a break for a few minutes.

However, the main difference that I really do appreciate is the flexibility, which I've previously mentioned. I'm in perfect control of my time and have the ability to spend it the way I want.

Running home-based businesses in the comfort of my own home gives a perfect picture of some realistic expectations with regard to work-life balance.

Everything was actually tough at the outset, from setting up to establishing a routine for work and family. Yes, I agree that there's a little flexibility, but work-life balance can't be initially expected, and can only be afforded once a system is successfully put in place for business operations.

I've just touched on pursuing passion and discovering your life's purpose. And being an entrepreneur is my choice, because that's where my passion is that I believe is aligned to my purpose.

I have always dreamed about doing what I want with my life by using the resources I have, for the people that I want to work with and care about, while making things happen for me that fulfills my God-given purpose.

Is there really such a thing as work-life balance?

It's hard to tell with certainty what the factual definition of work-life balance is. In essence, you have to look into identifying what work and life mean to you.

Work to me is anything that pertains to the professional aspect that includes business, career, or job. Lifestyle is how I spend my time with my family and friends for leisure and pleasure, self-development, spiritual nurturance, and other important aspects of my life other than work or career.

Work-life balance for me is the presence of achievement and enjoyment at the same time. Experts say that it is healthy for every human being to have that balance for personal growth and finding happiness and fulfillment in life.

## The Highest Human Good

A human being is a mental creature that makes us different from the rest of all the creatures in the universe. Our capacity to think rationally gives us the power and best advantage that other living things don't have; however, it can also lead us to our downfall when used inappropriately.

Our minds dictate how our lives really play out, affecting our moods, energy, attitude, and everything in between.

It is very common to hear from other people that happiness and fulfillment can only be achieved by a certain measure of success manifested by the amount of money, number of awards, higher positions, power, and fame. Don't get me wrong. These things are not bad. These are all amazing and may be considered by some to be their best achievements.

I don't want to judge people about their definition of what their highest good is.

As my life evolves every single day, I have discovered that what I really wanted as my highest human good is my own peace of mind.

On the surface, you may have imagined how literally chaotic my household is with four young children and the aftermath every morning. But really, I love the mess. It means I have people to whom I can express my love, care, and affection. I have beautiful human beings to serve.

To me, peace of mind is being able to connect with myself regularly and reflecting upon my very core to know who I really am and what I'm made of. It also means to being able to live in my now, the present moment, without having to lose my mind and worrying about anything. It is also about being able to not dwell on my painful past, judgment of others, and things I cannot ever control. In addition, it also means being able to be totally aware of my negative thoughts and actions, and correcting them when needed and never getting under my skin.

It is only when a person is at peace with himself/herself that true joy and happiness can be experienced, regardless of what the world is going through.

So, how can you possibly achieve your highest human good?

I suggest that you starve your negative thoughts and emotions, and draw happiness from within. You can definitely find peace of mind because you know exactly where the source is—YOU!

## Starting with The End in Mind

I've always believed that we were all created with a purpose, and everyone has to know what it is. We were given gifts and talents to help serve that purpose.

It's powerful to ask yourself first, "Why do I exist?"

And then ask this, "What am I really trying to achieve?"

We all want favorable and good results in everything we do. But the problem is, we don't have a crystal ball to predict or know exactly what will happen next.

Here's the good news.

By starting with the end in mind, you'll be able to manipulate the process because you know exactly what you want to achieve.

Let me explain further.

Beginning with the end in mind is simply fast-forwarding into the future and imagining what your presumed goals would look like. By doing so, you'll be motivated more by the future results rather than by the events in the past.

And imagine this.

How can you possibly know whether you've succeeded or failed if you don't know what you're aiming for? When there is a goal, you know exactly what target to hit.

I began to dream about my future as early as five years old. My brain was fed with different ideas by people close to me. And that greatly affected my plans through the years and in the process. Everything that I did was significantly related to the thoughts embedded in my young mind.

Although I cannot honestly say that my childhood dream worked out exactly the way it was originally planned, I was able to identify where my heart really is and how that is aligned to my goals, bringing me to where I am now through the things I've done and continue to do, which I will discuss next.

## Career and Personal Development

I have briefly discussed above about this concept, called work-life balance. And, again, to me, it simply means achievement and enjoyment at the same time.

All the successful people I know appreciate the value of being a lifetime student through mentorship, training programs, books, and other self-development avenues to upgrade their level of wisdom and expertise in their respective niches.

A guru once said, "Every master was once a disaster."

When I had identified exactly what I really wanted to do with my life through my passion and discovering what my life's purpose is, I started to look for ways to improve the God-given talents and gifts available to me, to amplify and enhance them, to nurture and grow them, so that I can bless other people as well.

In this world, we are given tools innate in us, but we are still the ones to decide whether to use them or not.

I may have chosen to be a stay-at-home mom, but I know it should not stop there. I know that I have all the freedom to use my flexible time as I should and improve to become the best version of myself.

I sought wisdom from my mentors, because the benefits are massive; no price tag can ever match. I fully understand that there's no shortcut to achieving success, but I know that there's a faster way to do it. And that's by copying the successful persons who you want to become and not repeating their mistakes, as well as learning from the lessons they've accumulated over their years of experience.

To succeed in life, we should accept the need for a lifelong process to learn, grasp new ideas for innovation, adjust to modernity and preferred future, and embrace the need for abrupt changes, so that we can become assets in our households, workplaces, and communities.

Personal development, on the other hand, is the pre-requisite to achieving career development, so to speak. We should always look towards improving ourselves first, so that we can contribute to the progress in our career or business. We can never take advantage of our human capital unless we enhance our skillset, knowledge, and experience.

When you develop and equip yourself with education—not just from schools, but also from self-help tools and training programs—it can also increase your net worth. Because I know that money matters to you as it is to me.

## Money Matters

I'm not quite sure if it's just a cultural orientation, but I grew up in a family where women were only confined to the house and were the ones managing the budget to run the household, while men were responsible for making a living. However, it became obvious that, because of the financial crisis and inflation, women also joined the workforce to create more income for the family. Either way, women or moms are still in-charge of managing the finances. Although this may not always be true for every family due to lifestyles and preferences, women are most likely the accountants in the house.

I initially thought that having an entrepreneurial mindset is inherited from one generation to another, but it wasn't true in my case. I've mentioned that I never had any family member with such thinking or mindset. When my late grandmother asked me for help to sell vegetables in our neighbourhood for a commission from the total sales, I felt joy, only to realize that I'd been seeded early on about entrepreneurship.

Yes, I may have enjoyed being an employee at some point, but I transitioned from the corporate world to becoming a business owner and being my own boss.

In the process of being a business owner, I learned about the power of leverage. Through some self-development programs and workshops, I was able to gain knowledge and wisdom that I now apply to every opportunity I encounter.

In my heart, I fully believe that every mom wants to stay with her family at home, and it will not make her think twice to leave her job, only if she knows how to start a business or any opportunity to earn money from home.

I'd actually written a book just recently, called *Mommy Means Business©*, which talks about maximizing one's earning potential while running the household. I have shared my businesses, which I run from the comfort of my own home while enjoying the luxury of attending to my family's needs, 24/7.

You can check the link here to buy it online:

http://mommymeansbusinessnow.com/

Whether we like it or not, we have to admit that money really matters.

We know that almost every decision we make every single day is dependent on how much money we have or don't have.  We may also have been sold by the line, "Money can't buy happiness," which is the same line I got my inspiration from to come up with the title of this book, Mommy Can Buy Happy Nest. Think about it for a second...

What if one of your children wants to go on a field trip, but you have no funds available for such?  When you examine closely, it's not actually the money that makes a person really happy, but the experience after the money is used.

Growing up with little to no money while my parents were struggling so hard to make ends meet, I began to not believe in the value of hard work.  I know I've already mentioned this previously.  Because, to me, if hard work really pays, why were we poverty-stricken?  Why did my father have to leave and work a thousand miles away from us?  No money, no dad?  In the back of my mind, there must have been a better way.

When internet was not easily accessible yet, I sought knowledge through books about leadership, self-development, and entrepreneurship.  Subsequently, I became involved in small-scale businesses, multi-level marketing, and other networking groups that taught me the art of selling and closing deals. These skills all made me more confident in pursuing my interest in businesses and entrepreneurship.

I was even inspired to know more about money matters when I read *Rich Dad's Cashflow Quadrant* by Robert Kiyosaki, an American businessman and a well-known financial literacy activist and speaker. He is also the author of the very famous *Rich Dad Poor Dad,* which is a financial book, considered to be the number one personal finance book of all time. This book challenged and changed the way millions upon millions of people all over the world thought about money, and I am one of them.

Whatever the case may be, believe that your life cannot move forward until you do.

Ultimately, a woman who manages herself, her family, and others well is a happy and a fulfilled woman through the three secrets I have revealed in this book.

If I can have it all, you can surely have it all, too!

*"Let' NOT fear stop you from being the best version of yourself and fulfilling your God-given purpose."*
— Anna Santos

## ABOUT THE AUTHOR

# Anna Santos
Author of **Mommy Means Business©**

Website: annasantoshub.com

Email: annasantoshub@gmail.com

Alternate email: annasantos2910@gmail.com

ANNA IS A MEDICAL LABORATORY TECHNOLOGIST BY profession and a Medical Transcriptionist for over 20 years. She had always wanted to become a medical doctor since age 5, a journalist, and a businesswoman at the same time. Although being the former never came to pass, she was able to roll her three dreams into one by putting up her own home-based business in early 2014, Trans-ACTS & Communications, which is a Medical Transcription company that serves healthcare professionals globally and now expands its services to diversified customers in the legal field, academics, media, authors, business owners of all trades and sizes.

She is happily married and a busy mom to her four amazing kids, which led her to leaving her corporate job to officially becoming a Stay-At-Home Mom (SAHM) in 2016. Apart from her very important roles she plays in her household, she is also known to be a "Serial Mommy Entrepreneur" who runs several businesses in the comfort of her home, and received nominations and awards for such. She had been featured in media and local magazines as well, including Canadian Real Estate Wealth Magazine. She is also a Real Estate Investor, a financial literacy advocate, and a life coach. As a result of the major transition she had made from being a corporate employee to becoming a serial mommy entrepreneur, she finds balance and happiness in all that she does that she now willingly shares to fellow moms and dads in the world through her speaking engagements, personal coaching, self-development programs, and the articles and books she had written and plans to write in the future. She recently wrote her latest book, MOMMY MEANS BUSINESS, which is now available on Amazon and in the major bookstores in the Philippines.

She also had the opportunities to share the stages and co-author books with the legends such as Brian Tracy, Jack Canfield, Kevin Harrington, and much more.

Her advocacy is for every woman and mom all over the world to find the beauty and power in her, that she is already equipped to make things happen for herself and others.

Connect with Anna now!

Anna Santos
Making Things Happen.